MW01109099

"Things I Have Told You"

"Take a Scroll and Write About...

Things
I Have
Told You"

Jeremiah 36:2

Discerning Your Journey

By Attention To Its Design

Virginia M. Winters

Winters **Wp** Publishing
Wichita, Kansas

"Take A Scroll and Write About…
Things I Have Told You"
Discerning Your Journey By Attention To Its Design

ISBN: 0-9661900-2-5

Library of Congress Control Number: 2006903660
Winters, Virginia M. 1920 –
"Take A Scroll And Write About…
Things I Have Told You"

Published by:
Winters Publishing
PO Box 782041
9350 E. Corporate Hills Dr.
Wichita, Kansas 67278-2041

Printed and bound in the United States of America

Editor: Samuel J. Winters
Illustrations and Cover Design: Dee Dunlap, Netwerks Creative
Photography: Ze Farha

Acknowledgments

Among endless of thank yous, special thanks goes to Bill Beachy, Al Durrance, Richard Foster, Mary Jo Grant, Morton Kelsey, Suzzane and Bob Layne, Benny and Earlene Mevey, Peter Osterlin, John Pruessner, Phil St. Romain, Essie Sappenfield, Cindy Snider, and Mark Williams.

To husband Dwight, my partner; son, Randy the builder; son, Dennis the teacher; the endless love of Mother and Dad.

There wouldn't be this book without the immeasurable gifts and persistent insistence of my son, Sam.

To all the wonderful people who have been and are still a part in the great weaving of the tapestry in my journey with God, that I could not mention due to the volume of pages it would take, I give you my heartfelt thanks.

Preface

I awakened long before dawn with a cluttered mind and heart. Confusing questions cluttered my whole being. Where do I go now? How do I know what you want of me, Lord?

I dressed quietly, left the house and walked in the dark before dawn to St. Stephens, a beautiful cathedral-like church nearby.

The silence, beauty, privacy with His Spirit welcomed me as it had other dawns like this...other day-breaks.

I knelt in a center pew facing the stain-glassed images of Jesus above the altar.

Ahh - the peace. The clarity of dialogue in Spirit. Where from this plateau? I see crossroads and many choices. Which way for me now?

In a while, dawn peeked through the silent images. I shared all with Him. I listened. Waited. Expected?

"Take a scroll and write about things I have told you."[1]

I will.

I am.

He is.

Through that a memory came;

"I join myself to all of Israel, to those who are more than I, that through them my

---

[1] Jeremiah 36:2

thoughts may rise, and those who are less than I, so that they may rise through my prayers."

This is the motion of growing together in Him.

I join hands with all of you, to those further along in their journey, so that I may rise to higher ground and those behind me that they may come through their valleys to a greater summit.

It is in this sense of sharing along our common walk that I offer my discoveries in the Spirit to sift with yours.

Virginia M. Winters

Chapter Summaries

When God first thought of me
And held me in His hand,
He breathed His hope and dreams in me
And formed a grain of sand.
He placed me there along the shore
With millions just like me,
Neath trampling feet and surging seas
I wondered if I'd be.
Yet He knew well where I'd belong,
If time and tide I'd bear.
And then one day
I glimpsed His plan
Through cracks in my despair.
I've known since then
Inside my soul
More so as times unfurl,
The pounding surf is just a shell
The sand in me a pearl.

"Things I Have Told You"

Introduction

Introduction

My first healing ministry was in our back yard woodshed when I was eight years old.

When the other girls played with their dolls, I had a clinic for dolls. I made medicine out of the dye from colored crepe paper, and the light shining from the windows through the bottles of colored water made a tremendous commercial. I really felt qualified to diagnose and treat my patients. I knew about treating the measles, chickenpox, scabby knees, fever blisters, and taking temperatures. Incidentally, every life was saved. They were all miracles. Nobody died. Every doll lived. Those were really, truly miracles.

As I grew older, I asked myself after reflecting on this experience, "Why did I want to heal the dolls rather than play with them? What caused that? Where did that come from?"

One of the first things I remember about my identity was my mother tenderly saying, "Virginia is the sickly one. She is my sickly child."

She lovingly and constantly gave me medications. All colors and kinds of medications because they would make me feel better. I was going to be well. It worked. I was well at six years old. Mothering consisted of tenderly giving medications for healing the body.

So there was a precedent for my clinic: the healing of bodies.

My second healing ministry came two years later when I was ten.

I remember because that's the year we moved into the new house, new neighborhood, new kids. It was pretty exciting till I cased a couple of blocks around. There were plenty of kids all right, maybe eight or so, but they were all boys. As if two brothers weren't boring enough!

"Cheer up," mother said. "Next week, we're going to Grandma's."

There was no place in the whole wide world I'd rather go than to Grandma's house. It was away, but still close - thirty miles. And I got to go by myself in the summer for a whole week.

It seemed every year there was a new discovery of serious importance at Grandma's.

This year, my tenth, it happened in the parlor. Now, Grandma's parlor was special. It was used only on rare occasions. There was a huge dark red brocade curtain in the archway dividing it from the dining room. If you peeked through, which I did every time I came, you'd see a door out to the front porch, then a library table in front of the window, with a big fern plant on it hanging down the side. In the middle was the big family Bible with a silver hinge on it. Beside it there was a sparkling oil lamp. There were two big dark stuffed chairs on each side of the table. Between the corner and the next window stood the Atwater Kent radio. Directly facing it, Grandpa's rocking chair. On the other side of the window was Grandma's secretary. On one side were all books behind a glass door and the other side was a closed desk and drawers. It was always locked.

This summer again I wondered, "What in the world was in that bookcase?"

When I asked Grandma how old I had to be to see the books, she said, "How about ten?"

They were mostly books I knew nothing about. History of countries. Bibles. Civil War books. On the fourth shelf there was a set of books called "The Russian Revolution." I took one out and saw pictures of soldiers with swords warring on horses. Chopped off heads stuck on fence posts. No, that wasn't it. Then I saw it. At the end of that set was the book. It was about three inches thick, reddish brown and old. One word on the cover.

I asked Grandma and she said, drawing her finger under the title, "Phrenology."

"What's that?"

"Read and find out."

I did.

There were pages of diagrams of the head from all directions. They were like maps, I thought. It described what all the lumps, crevices, and curves on your head meant. Every place in your mind and body was connected to your brain. Whatever was going on in your mind or body was controlled by the brain and that could be understood by noting the lumps on your skull. Know what part of the brain was under that lump and then you'd know what part of the body that it was in touch with, and you would actually know what was going on inside yourself. Amazing! An absolutely amazing discovery!

My whole week was absorbed in that book. It was the most exciting thing in the world!

"Yes," Grandma said. I could take it home.

My family lacked enthusiasm for my newfound world of knowledge; they couldn't have cared less. My brothers thought the whole book was "dumb." "Who cares?"

My Dad said, "Of course, honey, that's exciting. Go tell your mother about it."

Mother said, "Fine, dear, fine. Reading is good for you. Run along now. That's what summer's for."

"But, mother, this is miraculous!"

"I'm sure, and I want to hear all about it. But, not just now. That's a good girl. There, now. That's a good place to curl up and read. Get your feet off the sill."

What was I supposed to do? I had practically memorized the book of my life. It's mind over matter. I know all about it and nobody cares? What can I do with it? I'll think of something. I did. It took a few days to implement. But I did.

It took the rest of the week, but by Saturday afternoon, I was in business. I heard Dad come home, slam the side door and call upstairs to mother.

"Rita, what's going on in the back yard?"

"It's all right," she called back.

"What do you mean, all right? Virginia's out there with a dozen boys humming around. What's all right about that?"

"Calm down, Clarence," she said on her way down the stairs. "I'll tell you all about it…just calm down."

What she told him was, as I had told her, "There was no point in learning all this stuff and not using it. I couldn't use it without people to use it on."

I called on each house in the neighborhood, and told them my office would be open by Saturday at one o'clock. I promised that I could diagnose and prescribe. Everybody was welcome. The cost was one egg.

I went to Kroger's grocery and got some orange crates, some boards out of the garage, two chairs from the porch, pencils, paper, and lots of books. That made an office. I was open early.

It was first come, first served. As the patient was seated, I accepted the egg. I withdrew to the kitchen and separated the egg yolks, which I stored in the icebox for mother to use later to make Sunday custard. To the whites, I added splashes of water, squirts of Dad's cologne and beat furiously. Voila! The perfect hair-set solution.

All the boys came – some twice in one afternoon! I encouraged all the boys. (The girls had too much hair.) I brushed their hair straight up. Then with deft fingers, examined the terrain of their skull. Slowly, but thoroughly. Then came the diagnosis, often times showing details on my diagrams. I then prescribed various things but always with emphasis on the power in the brain to heal.

For example, Raymond. On examining his head, there were some definite irregularities. I asked if he hurt any place. Sure enough, his feet hurt. I examined a spot on his left-brain around the front area and there it was all right – trouble. He showed me his feet and no wonder! Both heels had blisters.

I told Raymond he definitely had sore feet. No doubt about the diagnosis. I also told him that the cure was in his brain. He didn't think right. "Think!" I said.

"First, when you get new shoes, remember to smash the heels until they're soft. Think about the size. Get the right size and they won't clop up and down. And most of all, Raymond, wear socks. Think about it. Use your brain!"

Raymond recovered and so far as I know never got blisters again.

Then there was Edward. His complaints were always a little unusual, but then, so was Edward. His head was kind of flat in front but interesting. He said he was nervous.

"No wonder," I explained and showed him on the map how that all came from the front, and in his case, the flat side of the brain. What he needed was more air.

"Think about it a lot. Every chance you get, get some more air. Don't waste time thinking about being nervous. Breathe. Breathe all the time. Practice. And come back next week."

I was sorry to raise his price to two eggs but his hair was so curly. One egg wouldn't even do all of one side.

Edward had a miraculous recovery.

By the time school started, I had quite a record of successes. To my knowledge, nobody ever got worse. No parents complained. Not even mine. (Only my brothers. Naturally they didn't want any more Sunday custard as long as they lived.)

On the other hand, I suppose there was one casualty. Me. I've never recovered from the fascination of that summer. Never.

In junior high school my English teacher was a small woman with full white hair, bunned on top of her head, and a little pince-nez on her nose. She would have us all stand beside our desks before class began and repeat, "You'll never know how much you know, until you know how little you know."

We would stand beside our seats until it was done well. No snickering, no boys rolling their eyes around, no girls whining; you would do it right if it took six times.

I was going to find out how much I didn't know.

In junior high our slumber party was the event of the week. We traded living rooms every Saturday night. We plopped on the living room floor in our jammies, snuggled up to each other in our blankets, and took turns sharing the highlights of our lives.

One night was rather solemn. Did they all know something I didn't? They did.

Beth Ann who had been chosen to speak for the group, said to me, "Would you please stop wondering about God. That's all you talk about. Junior high school is not about God. It's about boys, dates, makeup, and other important things."

Was I that weird? Must be. How could they not want to talk about God? I just didn't seem to fit in some how.

In high school my psychology teacher was Mr. Anderson. He really liked me. I stayed after school often just to talk. Sometimes he loaned me books from his own library. Besides, I noted one day, that he was handsome, tall, brown hair and eyes, soft gentle voice, and what a smile. I was in love!

It was a grown up kind of love, nothing like Bobby Turk in the back row. And then my world turned upside down. He married Pauline, the music teacher. After the school day was over, she wanted him to go straight home. I suffered in silence. I knew I would love him forever. My suffering did not begin to wane until after graduation. I suffered for over a year. However, the fascination with mind over matter continued all through school. Mind can heal body.

Turn left to college. My subjects were psychology and religion. Religion and Psychology. I studied everything on the subjects I could get my hands on. No way would I accept the proposed schedule for me. I'm here for psychology and religion and you say algebra? Are you kidding! I need all this other stuff for a degree? What happens if I choose my two interests?

"Then you're registered as a 'special' student.

"I'll take that."

The study of psychology and religion were both work and recreation, weaving in and out of life's usual progressions for the next ten to fifteen years.

And so it was, is.

The dark nights to come were actually leading into light, to the healing ministry that could not have come without it; the healing ministry of spiritual direction. The stories that follow are stories that define the transitions in the healing ministry of body, mind, and spirit over matter, to the Holy Spirit, over and in all.

"Things I Have Told You"

About Churchianity

About

Churchianity

Mother had said the first day after my birth was to church. All the weeks of my family's life pivoted around the church. That's what Sundays were for. They were predictable. Sunday school and church in the morning, then home for dinner. There would always be pot roast and vegetables, homemade bread and pie. After dinner, read the funnies with my brothers while Mom and Dad read the rest of the Sunday news. Dad usually folded his hands over the sports page across his middle and snored softly for a bit. Then every one into the car for a drive in the country. Home again in time for roast beef sandwiches, milk and back to church. Sundays were predictable. Sundays were great. Sundays rooted the week.

As I grew older, I helped with the little ones, then the junior choir, and taught primary school. By high school I sang in the senior choir and taught wherever needed. Sometimes *seniors*. Wow! Music and teaching were the joys for me. Not the rest. The preaching was always the same; the LAW. Law and sin. Sin and law. Though Sunday was *the* day of the week, it seemed separate from the rest. There didn't seem to be much relevance, except, of course for the things I would be guilty of, and that was for everything.

The only time I was in the preacher's domain was for marriage "counseling," if you could call it that. It took just a few minutes, a heavenly smile, and that was it. Mother was pleased. My husband to be didn't fare so well. Because of the rules, I simply could not, in good conscience, marry him until he was baptized. I had never been out of the church. He had never been 'in' one. As starry eyed as he was at the time, whatever I wanted was fine. Baptism, schmaptism. Whatever. Never mind his motive. In my legal system we were now to be "equally yoked."

The "yoke" continued in my new family by marriage in the same church. I continued as "church lady" teaching and singing; the children in proper classes; my husband, Dwight, pleased with this new dimension in his life. We were rooted safely in the church. Until, one Wednesday.

It was a usual weekday afternoon. The boys had just gone back to school from lunch. Dwight, who was in the wholesale tire business, had just made his usual mid-day call. I was about to leave for the grocery store when a car drove up in front of the house. Three men in dress suits got out and walked toward our door.

Who in the world are *they*? Ye gods! The elders of the church! I'd never even been close enough to speak to them and they're coming here? Yes, they were.

Did I look decent enough? Hair? Apron? Living room? I invited them in and "No," they didn't have time. They were on official business from the church. The words were confusing but there was no mistake about the message. Our membership in the Christian church had been revoked.

We had been ex-communicated. I was a "sinful woman." We were no longer allowed on the premises or inside the church building. The state of Kansas had voted "wet" and my father-in-law had applied for, and received, the first wholesale liquor license in Kansas. Liquor was against the law in the church so our family's position was sinful and intolerable. Furthermore, "This also applies to your children."

Then there was a dissertation on "the sins of the fathers," etc. They dropped our pledge card at my feet, dusted off their hands and left.

I remember looking forward to going to my church to hear the scripture and the sermons. Here I was in my twenties, with a husband, young children, the "white cottage and picket fence" and roses. All was looking good but, it was not to be so.

I died. The church *was* God and He had sent me away guilty as charged. I was abandoned, helpless and innocent.

The Church of my childhood was my lifeline to God. The church that someday was going to feed the forever gnawing of my heart. The preacher was straight from God and he knew the truth. He told me so. My church had condemned and ex-communicated us because we were all sinners, even the children.

My father-in-law chose this time to clarify his feelings too. I had never fit into his plans for his son. It was like trying to fit a skinny hand into a big boot. Now we were front-page news. His son was needed around-the-clock.

"Son will be with me working all the time. So you stay home, take care of his sons. That's all he needs you for anyway."

My health plunged. I was sick all the time.

Disintegration began in me.

All of me.

"Things I Have Told You"

About Healing of Emotions

About

Healing of Emotions

I was not at all prepared for a slide down the muddy road called "nervous breakdown." I floundered and clutched for rocks and trees all the way. I missed them all. I finally called for help.

I waited in the doctors' reception room for the psychiatrist. It was May, 1950, and I'm thirty years old.

I am in complete control of myself. It is difficult. Occasionally a feeling surges through, suggesting I collapse so that someone would lift me onto a soft bed and let me sleep. But, I dam this feeling quickly. No one in this waiting room here suspects that under this composure I'm tensely aware of controlling myself, every part of me

The room is quiet, clean and uncluttered. So quiet I could almost hear me tingle inside. The tingling, of course, is from concentrating so hard on being comfortable. My throat is very dry and aches. My hands are cold but, other than that, I'm quite all right – except for my ears. It sounds like they are glued to giant seashells. When I'm sure nobody is looking, I shake my head quickly. It clears some and I can see better.

It's necessary to keep very clear and in control until I meet this doctor. I must be alert enough to evaluate him accurately. I will trust him quickly. He must like me. He *will* like me. There wasn't a choice anymore.

I must not let my thoughts wander out of this room and away from this task of self-control.

"Virginia Winters." My heart took an extra leap when the doctor opened the door and read the top line of a brand new chart. It was a bit startling. I thought a nurse would call me. Perhaps he personally calls first time patients. I could see why.

As I walked toward the long hall he watched me. It wasn't obvious unless you were expecting it. In a sweeping glance, he saw that my shoulders were a straightened stoop, my clothes didn't fit, my heels were too high and seldom worn, my knuckles were white on my purse handle, my hair was curled too tight, my skin was dry and my jaw was rigid. I knew what he saw and I couldn't change it now.

He smiled pleasantly as I reached him and indicated I should follow him down the hall. In his office, he nodded toward a choice of places to sit. There was an examining table with a chair at the end of it; a chair at his desk and one opposite his desk. I chose the one opposite his desk. He took the chair at his desk and did paperwork or something that was no doubt unnecessary except in giving me time to relax and feel like nobody saw me. I saw him.

In a little bit, he asked me something but I wasn't listening so he repeated it and I said, "Yes, I was having a little trouble with my throat and my teeth." And, "Yes, I was tired all the time," and he just nodded slowly and I was able to continue with a whole assortment of aches and pains.

He asked routine questions about age, married, children, and so on. He asked me to hop on the examining table and he'd have a look at my throat. I was surprised a little that I jumped when he touched me. I wondered if he was. He examined my throat slowly and then my eyes and ears and I inhaled and relaxed. He smiled, excused himself and left the room.

A very pretty nurse came in and asked if I'd like her to help me get ready for a more thorough physical. I assured her I could do it myself. She smiled sweetly and said they'd be back in a few minutes.

There was a very thorough physical including blood work. And it was, oh, so soft and quiet around here. No state of emergency at all.

After the examination he asked me some sort of leading questions and I couldn't seem to think of anything except all my physical complaints. He asked if there was anything particularly troubling me. I said, "Nothing, except that I am a terrible person." I explained some of the ways I was a terrible wife, mother, daughter, and daughter-in-law. It seemed to boil down to that I just didn't do anything right for anybody.

"Was I afraid of anything?"

"No."

"Well," he said, in a dismissal tone of voice, you're in good shape physically. We'll give you a little something for rest and a little something for trembling and you come back a week from today and we'll see what we can do about some of these little fears."

I started to get up and then thought, what fears? I just said I didn't have any. I hesitated and looked at him a bit and I thought he was going to laugh. Instead he asked me, "What do *you* think is the matter?"

"I KNOW what's the matter with me," I blurted in my first natural tone of voice. "I literally give myself a pain in the neck!"

We both started to laugh at the same time. He had the deepest, friendliest chuckle I had heard in a long time.

He was kind of round – not fat, just round looking. He had very gentle hands, a rich voice, a bristly moustache and twinkles around his eyes like Santa Claus.

I felt he liked me kinda special.

After many months of umpteen office sessions came the hospital and insulin shock therapy. It is true, "Sorrows with their unshed tears make other organs weep."

It is also true, "There is no such thing as a disembodied emotion."

Healing was progressive and powerful.

When healing had blossomed through in a year or so, and I had passed the 'finals' so to speak, I was dismissed from therapy into my new life – one more than I expected or could have imagined.

In essence, he asked me to stay after class. "Would I be interested in researching some ideas with him?" Would I? I was so surprised, I thought I'd had a relapse. I said, "Yes."

So was birthed a new life out of dying.

I was part of the first known laity-led group therapy. We exchanged facilitator rolls with the same group and I compared, studied, and listened to his teaching.

He gave directions of what I should do or be. I followed his instructions and gave written reports.

A year later, he added occupational therapy for me with some of his patients.

Then chaplaincy training. Both with hospital chaplains and he as my mentor. I saw specific patients, formed new relationships. This was the icing on the cake.

Books appeared to re-shuffle; some old yet new again, some new bringing old truths into a new light – all stirring into the mix of these interim years. William James' *Varieties of Religious Experience* revealed thoughts not seen before as did the lives of mystics and the church fathers. Carl Jung renewed his appearance in my life but through a different door this time. Along side Jung was J.B. Rhine, of Duke University, and the fascinating research being done in para-psychology. Also, Frank Laubach's "profound dissatisfaction" with his life that birthed the classic, *Letters From a Modern Mystic*. C.S. Lewis again – this time I discovered more than words in his terms, "Christianity or Churchianity." And then J.B. Phillips reminding, "Your God is Too Small." And Harry Fosdick's – ahhh, the soother of my aching guilt with "there's more faith behind the doubts of men than in the practice of all their creeds."

At the close of our years together, he and the hospital chaplains had mentored me in several facets of healing in emotion, mind, and spirit. Those past years had given me the most amazing gifts of grace through Dr. Poling. The grace that waits for fruition in the lining of my heart.

An Accepting Church

In recalling the upheaval of uprooting family from its Church, came some chaotic times. Sorting out feelings allowed for some quiet perusal of incomplete longings. Mine was always for the Church.

The gnawing kept siphoning. After being ex-communicated from the Church of my lifetime, I had tried two others. They also said, "No."

Now, where?

My husband said, "Whatever, wherever you want."

Our kids said, "Wherever Jesus and lots of kids are."

One night at a party a new friend called out, "Hey, you guys, try the Episcopal Church. We take anybody."

"Even us?"

They did. We were in. Father John Pruessner and congregation welcomed us whole-heartedly into St. Christopher's Episcopal Church.

St. Christopher's was a new red brick edifice optimistically formed toward the edge of larger grounds to leave way for growth. The ground floor was sanctuary; the basement with kitchen and classrooms. Its massive front doors were flung open wide. The central act of Sunday morning worship was to commune with Him and be thankful. Sermons were shorter; heavy on grace and redemption and the Spirit of the law. (Church school was for extended education for all.) The symbolism, as aids to worship, did just that. The crucifix, candles, colors and vestments all heightened the panoramic view spanning today and "In the beginning, God…" Tender roots were replanted that day.

My doubts were acceptable. They sheltered my faith. Then the doubts had begun to dissolve and love of Christ in Church was allowed to come forth again. The love, in fellowship and sheer joy from the congregation and Father John absorbed us all.

I planted a new library. Dwight built a new kitchen, and the boys "met God." They called him the bishop. The bishop visited one Sunday. The priest was quieting the congregation for the Bishop's entrance at the back of the church. Our son, Sam, who was four years old, looked back and saw the bishop waiting to enter, dressed regally in white robes, holding a shepherds staff. He stepped out into the aisle, faced the quiet congregation and called out, "Here comes God!" We were blending in.

I knew homecoming. Why, I would understand later.

Ahhh, the stirring again. Now What?

After two wonderful years a business shuffle was transferring my husband to a new place, new town, a new state.

Will there be another like this where we're going? Will we be a church family?

"Things I Have Told You"

About Visions

About Visions

A transcendent experience during Easter Eucharist brings threat of expulsion or silence. It is mid 1960's in the Episcopal Church office.

The chapter establishes that ordinary people, like myself, are gifted by an extraordinary God. He calls us into experience with Him. Experience impels our search and calls us to confusion...

About

Visions

Easter I

Father John gave me some quiet times for pastoral counseling before leaving our home town for a new home in Ponca City, Oklahoma.

Where was I personally with my Lord? Was I where I wanted to be?

No.

The Holy Spirit living in and out of my heart was illusive as quicksilver. There was a place in me that was still restless. It was a gnawing hunger for God's close embrace. To have more of Him and less of myself.

Father John reminded me that next Friday night was Easter Even. Had I considered the Sacrament of Penance?

No.

Would I?

Yes.

After I learned from him and prepared myself, I was ready for my first and lifetime confession.

It was a beautiful calm spring evening. The small church was empty. Just Father John and me.

I was prepared. I knelt at the altar, facing the cross. Father John seated in front of me also facing the cross.

In prayer I saw my life in a fan shaped wake behind me. It came together in its point of focus in me that minute. It looked like the shower of a huge shooting star from its point trailing behind yet into me.

In another view, from my spot in the heavens, it's a sputter from a tiny star chip. From both places it matters. It is. It is my mark in the universe.

I watched its swath begin to break up from the hook into me and I wept. I wept for forgiveness, for pain I've left here, for sorrow from me, for love rejected to me and from me. Most of all for those you have called me into responsibility for; my family. Oh, God, I cry, how I cry. Forgive me all…forgive me each…forgive my self, oh, God, make it so, kiss it all, touch it all and make it well. I confessed my long list of sins, and some unknown just then appearing, deliberately, specifically. I received fully and gratefully the assurance of my forgiveness.

His hand became a great fan-shaped broom made of silk and golden straws and swept through the wake in one fell swoop and all was made clean; time and symbols spun into a process and were made whole. People in caricatures, like cartoons, were tumbling about in the wake like high-speed photography. They were people I loved. They were smiling. Being transformed.

His intentional will was fulfilled. I was forgiven...and forgiving mid wails and groaning tears that clung to the final whisk of the silk and gold.

I entered that moment clean.

It was a turning point for all of me. The Holy Spirit cleansed my body, mind, and human spirit. The pain I had felt was in the hunger for forgiveness. The Holy Spirit was given freedom to permeate all of me. The process of becoming whole was finally glimpsed.

On this night, I knew, at least for a brief moment, that there is wholeness. This is completeness. Hold on to, savor this moment. It may not come again, but His special gift will live in my heart.

I listened to His firm and gentle counsel and quietly left the church.

Outside I knew a sense of breathlessness, timelessness, stillness. The neighborhood houses and streets sat without a sound. Sun was resting in pinks and violets. Day was dying into life and so was I.

I watched, waited and a sense of peace and freedom began to well up and engulf me. I lifted my arms to the horizon, "Here I am, Lord, send me."

He did.

Easter II

The Experience

We settled in our new town, new home, new workplace, new schools, and a new church, the only Episcopal Church in town.

On Ash Wednesday morning the next year the usual small group, a dozen or so, had come for Communion. Father Bob was our gentle visiting priest who conducted Wednesday services. Father Maxwell, our parish priest, conducted all other services.

I knelt in the pew and looked up to the cross to pray. It looked different. It was a rich mahogany wood, but it seemed to have a luminous touch I'd not seen before.

As I knelt at the altar rail, it took on more of a soft brilliance. I was fascinated with whatever I was witnessing.

There was a hand on my shoulder.

"Virginia?"

It was Father Bob.

"Are you all right?"

"Yes."

"May I help you to your pew?"

"No."

As he helped me back to the pew, I realized Communion was over. Everyone had gone. The only lights were on the Altar. I gathered my things and walked slowly toward my car.

"May I ride back to work with you?" he asked.

"No. I'm fine."

"Do you want me to follow you?"

"No. Thank you."

I got into my car and drove to work. There was nothing automatic about it. I had to deliberately put the key in the ignition and turn it, placed my hands on the wheel, turned the wheels left, then right and straight ahead.

I felt very strange. I stopped in my parking space, opened the front door to the building, walked intentionally straight back to the stock room, sat down on a cot we kept there.

Dwight came back. "Are you all right?"

"Yes."

"You don't look like it. Want the doctor?"

"No. Call Father Bob."

I stretched out on the cot and soon after Fr. Bob arrived. He pulled a chair up close to me, said something in his soft voice.

"I feel very strange. Can you tell me what's happening to me?"

"I think so. You will be just fine. All you need to do is stay quiet. Stay still."

I did. I waited. I did not know for what but wondered what it might be. I was to wait.

So, I lay very still. I began to feel numbness in my feet, slowly rising to my ankles, up the calves, to my knees, through the trunk of my body. Then my vision faded and hearing dimmed. With the strange feeling in my head, I knew I was leaving my body. I had never heard of such a thing but knew it was true. I slid up and out.

I moved up about eight feet or so and looked down at my body. It looked very dead. My head was turned a little to the left, my left arm at my side. My right arm was across my stomach. Father Bob was holding my wrist pulse and sitting very still, very calm, just watching. I watched both of us. That ended as I became aware of where I was. I was in the midst of indescribable beauty; trees, flowers, hills, soft musical sounds, silent motion of living things. A place to learn about scriptures, mysteries, truths. All swirled around and toward me like a gently turning kaleidoscope. Seeing out of my body was being far more alive and real than seeing through it. Earthly life is finite. It is before infinite life. There was a voice teaching, but without sound.

The next familiar voice I heard was saying, "Nothing physical is real."

It was my voice.

"Nothing physical is real."

I was aware enough to apologize for sounding foolish.

"No, No," Father Bob interrupted, "I know what you mean."

I lay very quiet until I was where I had been a timeless space before. It was the next afternoon until I felt like my usual self: hearing, vision, voice. I was driving the car normally to work. There were some differences though. People, customers I knew, were more than I had known of them before.

There was a deep-seated joy and center in me I had never known. I would be listening to someone and see the Christ in them, a part of them I'd never even thought about. Then silently, I'd pray thanksgivings for them or their need. Then a scripture would surface like, this is how you are "in this world but not of it." Swirls of images would appear at times, images I now understood or could not yet grasp.

This lasted for several days and I occasionally felt a tug to go back to the church. On impulse I wanted to go, on second thought I was too frightened. But, there was a sense of incompleteness; this was not over. There is something else. I did go back several times but by the time I arrived I was frightened again, and began to tremble and shiver. Once I touched the door I became so terrified I ran. I knew that I had to go back, that I would. I was determined to follow through on this and finally, I did.

It was early in the morning. No one was there. The sanctuary was dark and still. The slate floor was cool, the cross was mahogany and the prayer benches were still red velvet. Everything was like it always had been. I knelt in the pew and said, "Here I am, Lord."

I folded my hands and prepared to wait...I don't know how long the silence was but it was deep and still. Then the mahogany began to tinge luminous. The whole cross illumined in a soft yet glowing light. Not like any other I'd seen. A dimmer glow filled the room.

A quiet sound began to permeate the loft like a far away echo of music.

The room warmed and his Presence was there. He was here. He knew me and called my name. I was no longer afraid.

I answered, "Yes, Lord."

The teaching began. This time I asked questions as comfortably as I would with my earthly father. He answered and even asked me questions about myself. I cannot consciously remember the bulk of the dialogue, but I'm sure it is blended into my soul. The time was closing. It seemed all that had happened crescendoed into an enormous smile; it surely was covering the world. I was absorbed in His Love; I was in Him and He was in me.

"Go in peace," He said, "Your faith has made you whole."

"Is there anything else?" I asked.

"I love you anyway."

The smile dimmed, the sanctuary darkened, the soft sound faded, and the cross was mahogany again.

I opened the sanctuary door to the morning outside: the colors of spring, trees, grass, flowers, the sky were more rich and glorious than they will ever be. There were diamonds in the dew. Standing before the wonder of it all, I knew for the first time in my life that I was not mine. I do not belong to myself.

I am not mine.

I am not mine.

After the wonder of it all settled in a bit I realized I would, or should, share the experience with Fr. Maxwell the senior priest. I'd at least try anyway.

Father Maxwell

"Keep your mouth shut. Get outta here!" He was furious. He was yelling at me! He was Father Maxwell, the church's senior priest.

Do I leave now while he's shaking his long bony finger at me or do I just sit very still until he calms down?

He seemed fine when I called for an appointment. What on earth caused all this?

"Every time you come in here you've got your head in the clouds."

What does he mean "Every time?" This is two to three times and those conversations were mostly about Acolytes and once about the kids' hayrack ride.

"Do you know what you do?" He was quieting some now. Drew forward the chair he'd kicked aside, seated himself and began to methodically arrange his desk top, mauling his words about.

Phone to right. Pens straight ahead. Spindle off the blotter pad, "Do you want me to tell ya? What you do is..."(rolling the calendar date)

"...You come to the altar..." (flicking the lampshade)

"...And then you..." He folded his arms on the blotter top, sunk his chin into his fists and whispered hoarsely,

"...And then you hypnotize yourself. That's what you do!"

He straightened as a Victor in the fray and said, "I'm sure you do it! You look at that Cross and hypnotize yourself, don't you?"

"No. No, I don't." I think that's what I said. I only knew for sure that I was scared and embarrassed.

I did say, "I just wanted to share something. It seemed at the time it should be with you."

"Well, I'll tell you this," he stood erect now, thumbs clutching his vest pockets and in his Sunday voice said,

"If one word of this gets around this parish, one word, you are out!"

He sat down, swiveled toward the window behind him.

I was dismissed.

Fumbling for my car keys, missed the ignition, so, just sat there, holding them in limp hands. Quiet. Humiliated? Yes, I was. I had an appointment with my priest to share a precious jewel with him. I had told him only the very beginning...Jesus had spoken to me, personally. Yes, He had, right there at the altar during Holy Week service. It was the truth, and he has a tantrum? Why?

He left the office. He left the room. He left me. It was more than humiliating. It was something like a child finding a purple rock in the mud, spit and rubbed to a shine. Cupped it secretly and run to mother with the secret of the year and she says, "Can't you see, I'm busy?!"

Not just like that but sort of. Feels the same. Something in me crushed.

Father Bob, our Wednesday supply priest believed me. He was there, wasn't he?

My husband, Dwight, tries to believe, to make sense of it. Strange things happen to his wife from time to time. He doesn't understand what I'm saying, but he listens. He'd be considered normal, whatever that is.

That's it. Seems like everyone I think would like to hear the good news laughs, shakes their head or pats mine, or just as bad, listens and checks to see if their watches are in sync.

Even my Mother, a devout religious woman, was nearly hysterical. "Oh, my God. Dwight, did you hear that? She thinks the Lord talked to her. Oh, MY GOD!" Clamping her palms to her forehead, "Call a psychiatrist. Call somebody."

My appointment was early the next morning. I was an emergency of sorts and that was all right with me as I was beginning to wonder myself if I needed a leash.

Dr. Jones was a member of our parish. I knew him from the holiday dances at the Club. But, he was a Christian, available, and really wanted to hear my story from beginning to end. That appealed to me. I was suspicious of his motives at first. (the bug under glass thing.)But, he listened intently, encouraged me further, asked few but reasonable questions. Even had a copy of

St. Theresa of Avila and asked if I saw parallels. I didn't, but was pleased to see this side of him. A sort of shared secret.

That budding rapport disintegrated at the door when he handed me "Six Ways to Reduce Stress" and a prescription for Valium.

Fr. Bob was my soul-friend. Twice he drove over from Tonkawa for an hour or so together. I remember the second time standing on the parking lot of our business stating that I honestly believed every body thought I was crazy.

"Do You? Oh, Lord," he cried. Tossing head back, arms high. "Oh, Lord, I should be so crazy!"

After great hugs, laughing, he hopped into his car, calling to me he said, "By the way. Won't see you next week. I have an appointment with the Bishop. Right! The Bishop, my friend, and we're gonna talk about this. See you the week after."

"Hallelujah! Hurry up! Can't wait!"

He never came back. (Months later someone said a parish had an opening for him in...I think Mississippi?)

When Father Bob was a few minutes late on our last Wednesday meeting, somehow I knew he wasn't coming at all. A sadness came. The sadness of endings. Maybe even the ending to this illusive mystery. Maybe, there is something wrong with me. S'pose? Oh, no, never in a hundred years could I imagine the Lord coming to me personally. Me? Not one such as I. To the Saints, the desert Fathers; the Holy people whose life vocation is being with Him. To the good and righteous, those people.

I didn't see myself as a bad person. No more than most. Just ordinary. About as ordinary as you can get.

I'm forty-three years old, five feet, five and a half inches, green eyes, one hundred and twenty pounds and blonde hair, the color of the current whim. I'm told I laugh and smile more than average. That's true. Also, I search for God more than most, at least, of those I know. I don't talk about that, but then others don't with me either. So, how would I know about them?

I live with my husband and three boys, and my mother is three blocks down. We're in the midst of the Great American Dream. We now had our own business; Skips Discount House, named after my husband's nickname. (Not like today where being in business meant you rent a space, haul in supplies, pack 'em back up and leave the keys in the box when the cash flow grinds to a halt. Not so in the 60's.) You buy ground, buildings, and inventory with all you can scrounge up. The whole family works; kids after school and Saturdays; Mom and Dad, six and a half, twelve-hour days. We drove a Chevy Malibu, lived in a three bedroom house, one-and-a-half baths, fourth down on the right, the red brick. You make payments on all of it and sink into a college fund. You belong to the business clubs, and Saturday night is at the Country Club to jostle with customers and competition.

Twice a year we go to market and Grandma corrals the kids. Oasis for me is in carrying lunch to my locked office, feet up, C.S. Lewis or Weatherhead. Smoke break area is stack of Laubach, Tournier and Reader's Digest with Menninger on family advances and personal hassles.   Then back to steam irons and invoices, etc.

The retreat in all this was with my neighbor, Pat. Late some nights we'd stretch out in lounge chairs in the back yard for a nite-cap. Dwight and Harold, Pat's husband, hashed the fish fry. Pat and I wondered who we were and where was God and why? Didn't last long - early Sunday and get my little acolytes in tow. Hair slicked and eggless chins.

You can see none of this was close to mountain top contemplation or sounds of silence in the desert that I experienced beginning on that Easter Wednesday communion.

Somewhere in all these musings I had moseyed on to work, parked in my spot and was staring at my desk calendar.

Dwight poked his head in, "How you doing?"

"Can you come in a minute?"

"Sure."

I told him about Father Maxwell and tried to tell him how far I had gotten into my story with him and I couldn't. I could not speak. I stuttered. I started again and stuttered. I was physically unable to say one word anymore about that Wednesday at the altar.

In the days that followed I made deliberate efforts to speak of it even aloud to myself but not one word could sound. Only stuttering.

Father Maxwell needn't worry about his congregation from me. At least, not for now.

I must wait. For what?

For how long?

I knew not.

And I waited for two years.

Easter III

The Gospel

The letter from Wichita informed me that the upcoming Holy Week Quiet Day would be held at St. James Episcopal Church sanctuary and would be conducted by Fr. John.

Fr. John? I hadn't seen him in years. Would it be possible to get some time with him? Any time? A few minutes? An hour? He would hear me. His reply to my request was affirmative.

"Yes," he would love to see me.

"Yes," there would be all the time I wanted. Hourly meditations would leave forty minutes of silence, which he kept also, with one exception. Me.

Father John had become our first priest and confirmed our family. He had always been there for us, in the best and worst of times. He was my first confessor; whether in the casual comfort of his study or the silent formality of the confessional, he heard me. And here he was again to hear my story.

When the time came to meet with Fr. John, I still could not speak of the experience. Being in a safety zone with him would ease that. Or, would it?

Rather than chance it, I borrowed a Valium, dropped it into my purse in a pinch of Kleenex. I took it within an hour of our appointment.

After greetings and chitchat we settled into comfy chairs opposite each other. I began by telling him about the convenience and habit of Wednesday Communion since last we met. I described the lovely Olde English church we attended and how, two years ago this Easter, I had stopped off on my way to work for Ash Wednesday services and ... the Valium was useless.

I made a couple of stammering attempts.

"You've had a religious experience?" he asked.

"Yes"

"Try again."

I did.

"Take as long as you need but continue. You'll be fine."

In another moment or so, the story began to flow again.

Fr. John listened attentively, re-lit his pipe only once. Now he tapped it in the tray beside him. Then looked up at me, smiling.

"Would you say I had a 'religious experience', I asked?"

"Yes," bobbing his head, "I would say that."

We sat quietly for a while. I was reflecting on my sharing with him.

"Did I miss anything?"

"Probably."

"Was it clear?"

"Probably."

I seemed to understand something else as I heard it again. If it wasn't all clear to me, how could it be to someone else? But, then, mystery was many faceted.

For instance, "How," I asked, "Could He possibly have said to ME, "...your faith has made you whole?" I am not whole and my faith, at best, is the mustard seed. How can there be 'faith' and 'wholeness'?"

"Right," he said. "You are not 'whole' and your 'faith' is seed size. But, that's all it takes. It isn't, how much? It's, where is it? In whom is your faith? The faith was in obedience. *That's* the action I hope you will listen to."

"He said, 'Come here,' and so you came. Faith is manifest in obedience. That's the action of faith."

"Obedience led to the 'wholeness'," he added.

"Remember when you said, "I was absorbed in His love; He in me. I in Him?" That was the wholeness. A split second in our time but eternal in His. The wholeness is in the abiding...the oneness."

"Does that help? You know, the decision to go back to the church?" he asked. "I would have flunked that one. I would have been so scared I probably would have gone back to bed, curled up in the fetal position...*that* was a scary thing to do."

"I was scared to death! What was that? Why the stuttering, the shakes?"

"AHA! It is a fearsome thing to fall into the hands of the living God!"

"Could this be *the* "fear and trembling"? Do you think so?"

"It certainly was "fear and trembling.""

"That's very helpful. Thank you," I said.

I didn't have a clue. "Certainly reasonable, not that it has to be, but it helps. Right?"

"Right. You'll probably have questions surface from time to time for a long time."

"The only one that is persistent, keeps nudging around, is His last words before the smile, "I love you anyway." Anyway? I've tried that from all directions. Did I miss something just before that? I just cannot remember. But it persists from time to time."

"I love you," I understand. But, "anyway?" I don't. I've tried it with different emphasis. I love you anyway. I LOVE you anyway. I love YOU anyway. I love you ANYWAY. What could I possibly have said that prompted His last word to me?"

Father John said to me, "Nothing. That IS the gospel; I Love you, anyway. No matter what. It doesn't matter what you do or don't do, in so far as my love for you."

"You are mine and I love you anyway. It doesn't matter if you go down into hell, I am there with you. I love you anyway. THAT is the heart of the gospel."

"So, I don't have to be worthy, read the right books, do the best deeds, be more than I am. He loves me, anyway."

And, that's the Gospel.

The Gospel that saw us through another shock. During a midnight storm lightning struck our buildings and burned our business to the ground.

We had one choice; move back to Wichita.

"Things I Have Told You"

⤚ **About Hunger** ⤙

About Hunger

This chapter shows how a taste of Him stirs hunger pangs - from gnawing emptiness to insatiable desire. A look at any newspaper's "Church Section" shows frenzied efforts to feed rebellion from empty calories and destructive hassle for "the bread." We *will* find satisfaction and, as in our physical appetite, even unto garbage.

The compromise chosen, between silence or expulsion, held promise and hidden mystery. Readers will identify with the appetite depressant of choice, a group who knows the *TRUTH*...

About

Hunger

"Even honey seems tasteless to a man who is full; but if he is hungry, he'll eat anything." [2]

Almost.

Therapy is incomplete without the spiritual dimension. Psychologist and clergy are both necessary. They include each other. They need each other. Of course, that's not altogether true if they are just repairing spare parts for a short term, but for healing that moves toward wholeness they are inseparable. Once we have surrendered to His Love, abided, and known fidelity, nothing else and no one else fulfills.

In the midst of an exciting work day, family birthday or the world series' ninth, a wave of emptiness, aloneness washed through me and, just as quickly receded to whence it came.

The longing is somewhat akin to a time in my earthly marriage and our separation in war. Watching the troop train chugging away through belches of smoke and screeching whistles while taking my husband around the curve and out of sight and sound...I thought I would surely die.

While a part of me waited with abated breath, most of me in both experiences moved on. Life just does go on:

---

[2] Proverbs 27:7

Life just goes on –

Sunrise, sunset

Laugh, cry

Live, die

Rest, run

Have fun

Eat.

Ahhh…food. The most crucial pit-stop down the pike is for food. Will they have my favorite? What sounds good today? Try something new or stick with vanilla? Will I even read the menu? Some are picky eaters, some ravenous meat lovers, some pig out on anything but all able bodies, out of conditioning and temperament, choose. Eating or starving affects all of me. I am an entity, not separate parts. So the choice of food is mine – therein lies fuel for the flame. My appetite snatched at every morsel in reach; scriptures, other books and my church.

My views had shifted with a new perception of hunger – teaching on hunger lit up for me. From time to time I called various places to ask if they had anything close to what I was looking for; a class on personal encounters with the Lord? Perhaps a study? Sharing? Even as I asked I sensed a subliminal message

– yes, there are places people could go to discuss their one-on-ones with God.

I chose to try one called Spiritual Frontiers Fellowship, an extension of the Church's Foundation for Psychical and Spiritual Research in England and founded by Oxford. (The nearest extension was JB Rhine of Duke University.)

An extension group right here in our City! And in a Church?

I called for a meeting date and appointment time with Pastor Newton.

Would I like further information?

"Yes, I would."

Would I like to come to his office for a chat? Get acquainted? What brings you here and all that?

"Do you have today off?" I laughed.

"Of course," he responded, "of course."

We settled into our purpose and exchanged ideas, feelings, doubts and experiences on the subject of parapsychology and related stuff.

I learned Spiritual Frontiers Fellowship was designed to bring people into community to share, study and experience frontiers of world of spirit. The world of reality that we cannot see with these eyes, to discover God's creation in that sphere so real, so mysterious, so full of promises – a deeper, close expression of Him.

Here in this fellowship, there are no foolish answers, no subject taboo. Everyone is learning and teaching.

Some upcoming subjects were angels, hypnosis, psychic phenomenon, spirit-body healing and more.

Some learned. Some questioned. Some bided their time. But, everybody listened. Imagine that!

"Yes!" I had a wonderful time.

"Yes," I would certainly be back.

This was for me. Not only could I learn from every subject mentioned, I had information to offer.

I opened my car door; I yelled, at the top of my lungs, EUREKA!!

The next gathering was a 'Welcome Home' for Rebecca.

She had been to a place called St. Brides in Aylesbury, England. There, a physician removed an enlarged inoperable tumor. Dr. Lang, and others, from the spirit world, performed the surgery through the hands of George Chapman.

She was absolutely radiant in sharing her experience with us.

I bought one of the books she had brought home entitled *Healing Hands*, by Dr. Lang. The subject was spirit-body healing.

I devoured it in a setting.

It was delicious.

I wouldn't have her experience; because that was in faraway England. I'd best hone in on all that I could absorb right here at home.

I was mistaken. Right here in the city came an unbelievable surprise under the Christmas tree, 1971; an envelope containing two round trip tickets to London for the third week in May 1972. The giver could not have possibly known about my interests or desires. As the original shock began to subside, I recalled Rebecca's remarks about the long waiting list! I wrote anyway and, would you believe they had one spring cancellation? Third week in May?

There could be no question about design in my journey. This plan was being executed. And I thanked Him. I thanked Him for this direction in my life, for guidance, that I would experience all He had for me, that I would know all of the unseen world in His will for me. The unseen was real and I was privileged. I thanked Him for all the steps along the way in these recent years that had led to this awesome possibility. The loving community of searchers had become my appetite depressant of choice.

"Things I Have Told You"

≋ About Channels ≋

About

Channels

In this chapter the reader goes with me to the banquet of experience, knowledge and fellowship of the group. And then, in 1972, through the unlikely circumstances leading from Wichita, Kansas, to Dr. Lang in Aylesbury, England, into my own spirit-body healing. These healers are real. I attest to that. Experience is a fact that may or may not hold more truth than discovering the elephant trunk but it is now a part of you and your formation for better or worse. My commitment to a Christian healing ministry begins here. The function of this chapter is to share the reality of this experience - not pros and cons. The group encouraged me to experience and study...

About

Channels

About Spirit-Body Healers

Spirit-body healers are real, whatever their defining. I can attest to that, having experienced them personally.

This story is an account of my time at St. Brides, Aylesbury, England, on May 22nd, 1972 through the spirit of Dr. William Lang in George Chapman.

I journaled this experience not to keep a record for myself for I doubt I will ever forget a second. It's as indelible today as it was then, but I considered that it would be of value to someone else someday.

I want to share enough of the highlights for you to discern its meaning for you. So, "Don't Touch That Dial."

This chapter is not about the pros and cons of methodologies or to persuade you one way or another. Later on I will show you my perspective from twenty years down the road. So, for now, watch.

Journal Entry 1972

As the plane roared off LaGuardia's runway I had not one qualm about the adventure I was beginning. I knew complete faith in this being God's will for me and was in submission to that will. What's to fear? My image of the world from childhood was still in view.

'God's in His heaven, all's right with the world.' He made everything; all there is and said, "It is good." Everything beyond my eyes was out there and He made it.

The world was three-layered; up there, right here, and down there - simple as that. God is up there watching me. The devil is down there stoking his furnace, watching for God's signals about me and my future demise. There was, from time to time, reference to the devil prowling around me up here, looking into matters for himself because he didn't believe God reported everything. There were, however, times I heard 'What in the devil got into that girl?' or whispers about uncle Ed's great knowledge of 'demon rum.' Other than that the devil had little to do with me, yet. Later was the dread time. All I had to do was 'straighten up' and 'do as you're told' by authorities in charge. These truths resting quietly in the depths of me saw no need to call out for discernment. My soul basked in sweet surrender form New York to London.

We touched down at Heathrow just as the Whitsunday Holiday weekend began; holiday weekends in England being Wednesday nights till Tuesday mornings, at least. My next Monday appointment with Dr. Lang at St. Brides in Aylesbury was an hour train ride west of London. Just minutes from our hotel in London loomed a daydream; Westminster Abbey. For a middle class Midwesterner in 1972, this was an impossible dream even for the deep-rooted English.

The Abbey stood majestically in the midst of tales of ancestors come alive for me on Sunday; I entered into the communion of saints inside those hallowed walls. I made my confession, was assured an absolution, offered myself, received Him in the holy Eucharist. At no time did it ever occur to me that I would be so blessed in preparation for the time to come.

It was here. My Monday appointment with Dr. Lang in St. Brides at Aylesbury.

St. Brides was picture book English; stone cottage, snuggled by flowers, flagstone walk behind a white garden gate complete with bell. Inside seemed very much like the ordinary American doctor's office; receptionists, magazines, leather chairs, doors with names. It was surprisingly simple until a door attendant opened one of the doors and announced,

"Mrs. Winters, from America."

The woman leaving was being wished a safe journey 'back home to India'. My husband and I stood, a quick hug, I handed him my purse and walked through the door.

The room was about a 9x12, dimly lit, if at all. A table and two small facing chairs sat at one end. A wash basin and towel rack were on the opposite end. Along side was an examining table and step stool up to it. Dr. Lang was at the basin scrubbing his arms and hands with his back towards me. As he began to towel his arms, he turned, and in high pitched, clipped English, said, "Come in, my deah, come in!" I was shocked at his appearance.

My eyes, adjusting to the darkness, could see that he was grinning from ear to ear, perhaps a grimace. His eyes were tightly clenched. His hair was quite gray, disheveled like a shock of Einstein. He finished drying his arms and greeted me again in his elderly voice. From a very old head on a body at least half his age; this indeed was Chapman and Lang, at last. An awesome sight.

As he walked a step or two toward me, I held my hands out and he took both in his. An instant shock of an overwhelming love surged through me. He indicated my chair and held my hands until I was seated.

The Interview

"I trust you're feeling better? We'll have you well in no time at all, my deah. Did your husband come with you? How did you enjoy your flight?"

"Mrs. Winters, we've been doing some long distance healing for you since February. Correct?"

"Correct."

"Has it been helpful? What is your condition now?"

"I can't say whether it's been helpful or not. There has been a change but I don't know what it means."

"What's the change?"

(A part of the preparation was in meeting by phone every Monday night in prayer at 9:00 p.m., our time. I was to be the recipient; be open to whatever was health-giving for me. And be thankful.)

During prayer time there is nearly always motion in my abdomen; pulling, turning, drawing. Not sure what it is. Sometimes I think the swelling has diminished considerably, but not always... So there is change but I don't know what it is.

Except for the unpredictable energy and endurance, no change.

A bit more along this line of questioning and he asked, "How old are you?"

"About 45?"

"No. Fifty-two." Now THIS was using typical American finesse. Or, was it universal?

"Well, now." he stood.

"If you'll stand, we'll see what we can do for you."

The Examination

He stood at my left side, put his right hand on the vertebrae at the base of my brain and very lightly touched my forehead with his left hand. He moved that hand very slowly down my face, barely or not touching at all, and touched various vertebrae at the same time. Just as he reached about the middle of my chest he stopped, held it, and then lifted it in a jerk and down again. Then he moved his hands very slowly all over my body, down to my feet.

About four times he stopped, and appeared to be listening or thinking; left abdomen, down towards the groin and then on the right side and back to the chest. Each time pondering, still smiling with eyes tightly clenched. Indicated my chair and we sat down facing each other.

The Diagnosis

(The following are excerpts from my journal written immediately following The Experience.)

"Your problems are several but we can take care of all of them."

"First. Your digestive upsets are coming from the pylorus. Do you know what that is?"

"No." (I would have guessed something about gums.)

"It's the opening from your stomach to the duodenum, beginning of the small intestine. It's like a funnel you might say, and yours is upside down. Your food is not prepared for the small intestine so it is not predigested. So it just plops. It plops into the intestine. This causes distention from undigested food and air pockets. We can repair that. We'll just turn it right side up - reverse it. Is that all right, my deah?"

"Second: Your pulmonary artery never developed from childhood. It is very small. It cannot carry the supply necessary for an adult body. This creates a lack of oxygen, hence the exhaustion, endurance, and fainting. You've never breathed correctly in your life. We can take care of that too. We'll simply enlarge the artery. Is that all right, my deah?"

"Third: your entire endocrine system is sluggish and will be easily corrected."

"Fourth: We'll remove (repair?) the mass(?) in the left abdomen and remove (repair?) the ileum. Is that all right my deah?"

(Several times I said I didn't quite understand and he explained it again. Because of his accent, I still did not understand. So, I thought, I don't know what he's doing, but he knows what he's doing, so...)

"Go right ahead."

Then he asked, "All right, my deah, shall we go to the table?"

He touched my arm, helped me up to the table and I lay down.

The Surgery

He walked to my left side and repeated the diagnosis and procedures. And, did I understand?

"Oh, of course. Go right ahead."

Then he walked to the head of the operating table, placed a finger lightly over each of my eyes, and said,

"Now take a deep breath, exhale...relax."

He slowly drew his fingers down from my eyes and face. I took a deep breath, exhaled, and relaxed.

"Now, theah's a deah guhl." He was pleased.

He walked back to my left side, was silent a few seconds. I heard bits of sounds like clicks and snaps.

Then a sensation like a fingernail tracing skin and in the shape of a banana on my left abdomen. (I was fully clothed).

I felt a deep peace and didn't know whether I was immobile from wonder or a kind of hypnotic anesthesia. I didn't really care, just a touch of curiosity.

Then he moved to my chest and the same procedure. It didn't seem quite as long as the first and the sensation was in a different shape. There was a sense of hovering motion all over my chest and upper abdomen areas. Then silence.

He touched my eyes and repeated the first procedure. My awareness diminished again. He moved to the groin and then to the right side but the motion seemed hazy and distant. Then he leaned over me, "We are finished and you are on the road to complete recovery."

"Before you get up we will replace your spirit-body. We carefully draw it away from the physical for repair and then replace it. It takes just a bit."

He began from the left side again and methodically went through the exact procedures as before in each area. The first time had been barely perceived, if at all. This time was not painful but there was firm pressure. He seemed so delighted he could hardly contain himself. He slipped a hand beneath my neck and said, "Sit up, guhl, sit up."

I did. He helped me from the table as though I were a fragile child. He slid me from the table, put his arms around me and touched my spine; every vertebra once and some two or three times.

He indicated my chair again and asked if there were any questions.

"Questions?"

I laughed, "What happened?"

"Well," he was laughing now, "let me tell you." And he did. Again.

Instructions

"Follow my instructions exactly."

"I will."

"When you leave here, go straight to your quarters, take a hot bath for about 15 minutes. Then, go to bed for about two hours. This will give the healing in the physical body a chance to begin. And then, if you feel up to it, get up in the evening and go outside. Within 24 hours you will have drawing sensations and there will be some twisting and churning about. DO NOT be alarmed because this is only the natural healing process. Do you understand all I've said to you?"

"Yes. I think so."

"One more thing. Diet. Stay on a high protein diet for three months and…"

(The instructions given me were exactly the same I had journaled following our 9 p.m. prayer meeting time in March.)

"I believe that's all, unless you have a question?"

"Not now," I said and as I turned toward the door I heard in a voice happy but near tears, "Goodbye, my deah. Goodbye my deah guhl."

I turned back to him and could not resist his open arms. As he held me close to him, the same overwhelming love surged through me. A fitting closure. Full circle.

The Aftermath

Leaving St. Brides, my husband and I decided to walk leisurely back to our quarters less than half mile away. Who could resist the beauty of a day in May in England? We could mosey along while I updated him. With the exception of stuttering over my own words, I felt much as usual. My healing did not begin in about 24 hours; it began in less than two blocks. I began to feel weak and trembly. Strange sensations in my abdomen; turning, twisting like the first stirrings of a child. It was obvious to both of us a cab was in order.

As soon as we arrived I went straight to a hot bath for about fifteen minutes and then to bed for two hours. My husband pulled his chair up beside the bed and we puzzled about the meaning of all this. What happened? What's next? I placed my hand on my chest and was startled that it was quite tender in the center. The tenderness spread rapidly like something being poured in my chest and became hot and painful. The pain increased, then leveled; we relaxed a bit. Then, began at that same level and intensified. We did not know what to do. Now, it felt like a raw wound, like the first awareness after surgery.

As we were trying to decide whom to call, it began to subside and seemed to slide back to normalcy. We thanked God for the healing going on and to come.

Then I drifted into a sound, uneventful night's sleep.

On awakening I quickly felt my chest. No tenderness. No pain. As comfortable as before. The surprise sensation was my face; it was as soft and moist as a young girl's! The skin beneath my chin and eyes was taut and moist. That was ME in the mirror! And I felt wonderful. It's over!

After a hearty breakfast of scotch eggs, ham & muffins & jam, we decided to stay on another day or so and take a run up to Oxford while we were so close.

It was a beautiful bright spring Tuesday in Aylesbury and the bus station was just two blocks up the way. What a delightful idea for closure to this experience.

Delightful, indeed, until we boarded the bus. A drawing sensation began in my groin and left side, like a puckering feeling. The pulling would escalate and then subside... rest a bit and begin again. At our first stop, I stood in the aisle and recalled this same feeling the first standing after birthing. Our day at Oxford was like none other.

By Thursday I was so completely symptom free, we decided to catch the early train back to London. As my energy was bounding now, we decided to get off short of Victoria Station and have a good sightseeing walk. I could not believe where we were standing in less than five minutes; right in front of the *Church's Foundation for Psychical and Spiritual Research*! I had read and heard much about their work in Spiritual Frontiers, their U.S. extension of the foundation, and longed for deeper understanding. I had even seen pictures of this place, but to be here, looking at it? Of course, it was Friday and the sign said CLOSED. We stood there a while and I told my husband of some of the work done there and going on now. A man walked around us, up the walk to the steps, unlocked the huge scrolled door, turned, smiled at us, and said,

"We'll be open on Tuesday. Does that help?"

"Not really," I said, "We'll be leaving on Tuesday."

"Where are you from?" he surmised.

"The states...Kansas."

"Oh, really. Could I help you with something straight away? I just came down to check the post."

"Could we just take a peek inside then?"

"Of course. Come along."

He introduced himself as the Secretary General of the Foundation and was so enthusiastic about giving us a 'peek' that he toured us from floor to floor and hours later in the day he had answered everything I ever wanted to know about their research and didn't know who to ask.

He interviewed me about my experience in great detail and with such expected professionalism. I hadn't the slightest idea how he thought about it.

We left with great hugs and promises to stay in touch.

And, I, with great thanksgivings to the Lord for all He is showing me.

I threw away all my pills before leaving for Scotland. We traveled the rest of England and down to Paris. I ate whatever I wanted every place, walked miles, flights of stairs, prowled castles, even a twenty-four hour flight home out of the inevitable control tower strike in Paris. Not one problem with digestion or energy.

While waiting our long turn on the runway I pondered the power; the immeasurable power available... such easy access! People should know about this. EVERY body should know. As we zoomed through the clouds and into the blue, I knew. I knew why such a precious gift for me, at least through the glass dimly.

I knew I was to study healing within the structure of the Christian church. That was it. With all my heart and soul involved, this was my purpose. Learn all I possibly can. But, why? To do what with? I don't really know. Maybe to share? Maybe a link someplace? I just don't know why. I just know that's it. Maybe I'll be an instrument. I give you all I have, Lord. For sure, I know, all things come of thee, Oh, Lord, and of thine own have I given Thee.

Home

Names and phone numbers to call "the minute you get home" were still in the their place.

First was Shirley.

"Hurry. Come for coffee. Now." I did.

We did celebrate healing in England. On leaving, I noted a magazine tossed on her coffee table. *Sharing: A Journal Of Christian Healing.* Published by Order of St. Luke the Physician International.

She did not know where it came from nor did she have the slightest interest and…

"Yes, if I did, take it along!"

This was for me!

There were articles on Christian healing, resource persons, book reviews, calendar of events and a list of "Chapters in Your Area."

Within the hour my query was in the mail. I watched it slide down the shoot and knew I was right where the Lord wanted me, doing exactly what He wanted me to do. I knew it for sure. Certainly for this lane of the highway.

About Mediums

In the same mailbox, same day, mail came to me. I was invited to participate in a séance. While I'd read and heard about séances I'd never seen or been involved in one, till now.

The callers said the woman was coming through Wichita on her tour from England to Hawaii. She would conduct the séance on the following Sunday afternoon in the caller's home and have a dozen people and then be on her way. We were quite privileged as she was considered one of the best in this field.

"Yes," I could be there. I could hardly wait!

I went straight from the phone to my bedroom, closed the door, picked up my Bible and sat down on the bed and prayed something like this: "Thank you, dear Lord, for this chance to see you unseen. Help me to pay close attention – to not be distracted by the process or mystery of it all – just to learn and see all you want me to see."

Sunday was a bright, shiny day in sharp contrast to the home of the great event. All drapes were drawn, dimmed lights, quiet voices. There were one or two introductions but most were from the group. The medium, as she was called, was a very warm gracious person, rather shy, gentle woman until time to gather 'round table in the next room. Lights were off, candles lit and silence prevailed as we sat down and joined hands.

My heart seemed to leap with anticipation as I reminded the Lord, "Show me, Jesus. Stay with me, Jesus. Don't let me miss anything that's for me."

Candlelight flickered on quiet expectant faces. The medium's eyes were closed, her demeanor changed from softness to firmness, her features seemed fixed and still like a corpse. She began to speak softly, inaudible to me. Then clearly addressing another voice, the other side, she seemed to be speaking to persons known to her. She spoke to them awhile in a monotone that seemed to draw all the others into a state of twilight or dozing level, including me.

In a while, I didn't notice how long, she invited someone specific, calling by name to come, to stand before us with the message. Silence. A second time she called. Silence. The she spoke some unfamiliar words that accelerated to a command to appear. Silence.

Surprisingly, she then spoke directly to us in her normal voice, admonishing us to clear our minds, to concentrate on the experience at hand and a few other comments including "We shall being again."

Begin again, we did. Same procedure and unfortunately, same results. I wondered how many times it would take for someone to materialize. (In movies it was the first time.) There was, what seemed to me an uncomfortably long stillness until she said, "This will be all for now. There is some chaos on the other side — some disruption. I am sorry."

She rose from her chair and said, "This is my first failure."

I went straight home, to my bedroom, and told the Lord how disappointed I was. This one great chance ever and just nothing. Nothing, at all. I told him I was sorry I didn't see what he wanted me to see. He didn't answer. At least I didn't hear till later.

With séances fading behind me there was remembrance of still another time. This one completed my association with the group. The Christmas party.

Edna called after Thanksgiving to say, the rest of the group was sorry I'd not been able to attend meetings regularly since my return from England. They'd s'posed we'd see ever more of each other. It was true, I realized. I'd attended probably twice since sharing my story, but I was just busy with other directions. Possibly next year would be different. (Indeed it would!)

She wanted also to remind me of the Christmas party. This year, nothing serious, just some good fun. Bring a Christmas snack and your ouija board. Ouija board?

"We thought it would be fun to have several working at one time."

Fun? Ouija boards? I'd had one experience with a ouija board. Somebody gave mother one when my brother Jim was overseas in World War II. She read the instructions, placed her finger tips on the planchette and off it went, gliding across that board and to her absolute delight when she saw, "Hi mom. It's Jim. I'm fine." She had an instant hook.

She 'ran' (as she described it) that board at least every evening and many days. She was a widow alone and Jim talked to her constantly. Usual phone calls to me were, "I just talked to Jim and he said..." It was always good news. "Feel fine. Be home soon. No danger."

Occasionally, a bad report about his health or imminent danger was proclaimed. For the most part it brought her much peace.

I never for one minute thought she was hearing from anybody but herself. She heard exactly what she wanted except for the fears, that were easily dealt with. They also, I believed, were projections of her own mind.

She wanted so for me to have such consolation. And, I wanted her to believe we could share this. It simply would not move for me. The touch of my fingers seemed to seal the planchette to the board. Mother would start it and then tell me to "hop on now." I did. It stopped. It would be racing for her and one of my fingers on would stop it. She was truly sorry for me and concluded I just couldn't connect with spirits.

"It's a gift, y'know."

I would think a ouija board party was fun? I thanked Edna but, "I already had a commitment on the party date."

That was it.

What had happened since my first enthusiastic meeting with the group? Where was the spiritual research? Where was the spiritual?

It was a long way from my now consuming curiosity in the Order of St. Luke. Today's mail brought

Sharing magazine with the page noting new "Chapters in your area."

Finally, the day came bringing firm direction in the pursuit of Christian healing, the day laid the path toward those people who would teach about discernment on my journey and spirits along the way.

The direction was on the chapter news page in *Sharing*. At first it looked like there was no place for me but as I finished scanning the page, the bottom line read,

"If there is not a chapter in your area perhaps it is your mission to start one."

That's it! Let's go!

Start one? Me? How?

"Contact your regional Warden listed on page nine."

Kansas was the northern of a five-state region. The Warden's office in Arizona. My query letter dropped down the same slot as the first letter that very afternoon and with the same satisfaction; this was my direction. I was exactly where He wanted me to be.

"Things I Have Told You"

About Christian Healing

About

Christian Healing

Order of St. Luke The Physician

The Order of St. Luke the Physician is the study and practice of Christian healing. It does not isolate you, insulate or elevate you. It does identify you. It is who I am. My corner in the Kingdom. My little niche in His Body. It permeates my life.

"The greatest growth of the Church of the twentieth century will come about by the return of the healing ministry to its proper place in the church where it began." That was the conclusion of the bishops of the Lambeth Conference of 1930.

Out of that conference came the Fellowship of St. Luke. It increased throughout England and the English provinces and came to the United States of America in Bakersfield, California, and was founded by John Gaynor Banks in the Episcopal Church. At that time the Fellowship was renamed the order of St. Luke the Physician. It quickly spread ecumenically and is now become worldwide.

About

Christian Healing

Order Of St. Luke The Physician

I applied for and began my novitiate with great gusto. The first requirement called for a clergy/chaplain. Fr. John Pruessner volunteered for both.

The second called for five members committed to prayer and study.

I spread the word of OSL going to many places and spaces. I went out knocking on front and back doors of churches, proclaiming the healing ministry of Jesus Christ belonged back in His church, where it was in the first place. I found clergy who had stories and interests to share and had kept their secrets of divine encounters of healing from their parishioners; the Churches had more closets than I knew!

I would never have thought this would take two years; two years of constant contact and awareness of possibilities at every gathering in the church. The outcome of my efforts was the formation of an enthusiastic group in my church St. Christopher's. I volunteered and was "elected" to be the first convener.

The people of St. Christopher's also admitted having a hunger to experience more of Christ. The healing ministry would be direction to satisfy that hunger.

On a Sunday morning, the priest asked me to share my England experience just to get the congregation's response.

Responses were mixed. Some were in awe of God's work. Others thought it was all my imagination. Others scratched their heads not knowing what to think. But, the experience was accepted by all to inspire the study and practice of Christian healing.

The best news in this time was in learning about the healing ministry of the Church actually going on throughout the world (OSL was international) and the work written by its dynamic leadership, leaders whose work was recommended or required!

Discernment of Spirits

Dr. Alfred Price was the international Warden, who through his ministry became a living icon to me. From his beginnings in St. Stephan's, Philadelphia, which had become a Mecca for healing in the United States, to the vast and available library, I was beholden.

While studying his work, even in moments of sharing deep insights, I never for a moment thought about actually meeting the man personally. But, I would. According to the OSL news he would be teaching in Kansas City, just two hundred miles or so up the pike, in early fall and just before our Wichita chapter would finally begin. Such timing!

To hear him, especially at this time of beginning would be such a booster shot. To maybe speak with him was even a possibility? If that should happen if only for one question, it would be about England. He would know. I had quietly put it away with Easter. I had not and would not bring it out again till it was understood. Some discernment from Dr. Price was almost too much to expect.

So was the guest arrangement in Kansas City. Would you believe we were assigned the same hotel, rooms next to each other, the same courtesy car to and from the conference? True. Also, true, I was absolutely tongue tied in this presence. He was a big bear of a man who laughed heartily and kept up a fascinating, and for the most part, a one-sided conversation.

During teaching sessions he kept a question/comment box nearby and after breaks would answer them before continuing his subject.

That afternoon I slipped mine in. "Do you believe a deceased person can enter the body of a living person and work through him?"

He read the question. Smiled at it. The room snickered and chuckled. He looked up and smiled.

Embarrassed, I looked straight ahead. He said, "And the next question…"

On the way home he turned to me in the back seat and asked, "Who do you think our spiritualist was?"

"Spiritualist?"

"Yes, the person who asked about the body possession."

"That was me."

"You?" He looked straight into my face. "Really?"

Silence.

The next stop was his.

The car stopped. The door opened. He got out. The moment had come and gone.

Dr. Price's encounter caused me to question the discernment of my journey to England again.

Spiritualism? The term had never entered my mind. How awful. The séance sure smacked of what little I knew about spiritualism, although it never occurred to me at the time. But, England? That was entirely different. Or, was it? If so, then it was not Christian. If not Christian, why was I so sure it was His leading? How about the love? The healing itself? What's going on here?

Another person to have a deep impact on my discernment journey with spirits was Rev. Jim Johnson[3], a much revered Methodist evangelist. He and Francis McNutt were conducting a healing conference at Oral Roberts University in Tulsa, Oklahoma, and our OSL chapter, which had been going full steam ahead for years by now, was attending.

During a break time I had met with Fr. Farr, the Vice-Warden of OSL, to invite him to Wichita. I asked if he could counsel me on the séance experience or refer me to one of the many clergy and therapists attending. He said,

---

[3] Pseudonym

"Interesting. Jesus called His twelve disciples together around the table also. Perhaps another twelve were called and you were the Judas."

"Hadn't thought of that. It *is* interesting."

Then I gave a very brief description of England. Could he help?

"Wait here," he said.

"I know someone who can."

In a few minutes I was sitting back stage on the bleachers face to face with Jim Johnson. I never would have believed it. In the midst of a multitude of people I was alone with Rev. Jim Johnson. He made me instantly at ease with my story of six years ago still haunting me.

He listened intently, concentrating on my eyes, and without a word till I finished. Then he took my hands, closed his eyes and said,

"Now honey. What matters most is the movement." Opening his eyes he asked slowly, "What direction did it take you?" Closer to the Lord or further away?"

"Closer to the Lord."

"Good," he said. "That's the most important. Now, did you accept the method?"

"I don't know. I guess I didn't question it. At least at the time."

"Did you," he asked, "accept what you thought was a gift from God?"

"Oh, yes. I sure did."

"Now. I heard in your story that you felt led to prepare and did praise and thank Him."

"Yes, I did."

"I have to say, that I'm not one who lumps all these off as the work of the devil. God uses him, too. God uses the devil as a stepping stone sometimes. Maybe the young Dr. has moved more toward Jesus. Ask him."

He stood up and as I did he gave his special brand of bear hug I'd heard about and said, "He loves you very much to protect you so much. Accept your healing and praise God. You had a close call."

Then he laid hands on my head and prayed with authority for my cleansing, emptying and infilling...and it was so. I felt a sense of joy, peace and thankfulness.

It had never occurred to me before that God always honors our motives. He leads through those too. Like we accept a child who drops the glass of milk while offering it to us; our mistakes don't matter if you reach out for Him. This was a new insight.

Also, was the devil involved? Apparently, Jim Johnson thought so as others had implied too. That even if the devil was involved the Lord used him for his purpose. I don't know why not; "Greater is He who is in you, than he who is in the world."

I was to learn an even deeper, wider truth.

Healing Prayer Teams

One afternoon I went to the office of a group of women called the Mothers of the Disappeared. I spoke to a woman named Rosario who told me her story. Her husband, four children, and a grandchild were killed by the Salvadorian security forces.

"My life is like a necklace," she told me. She pointed to a wall piece reading;

Do Not Forget

In a Fabulous Necklace

I Had To Admire

The Anonymous String

By Which The Whole Thing

Was Strung Together.

Bishop Camara[4]

"The bead would have gone rolling all over the floor with the suffering I've experienced if it weren't for the work I do, The Mothers Of The Disappeared. God has given me this support group which is like a string that holds the beads together."

It was also our day for ministry to infants. A ministry for OSL through Claudette who, with Children Services, cared for babies from birth to adoption.

She would bring a new baby several times for 'touch, word and things!'

These team times were prayers for healing of memories, birth process, womb, conception and

---

[4] Brazilian Archbishop Dom Helder Pessoa Camara on commitment to the poor.

generational healing. All areas of study in OSL that we were beginning to put to practice.

They were loved, anointed and sent on their way.

Today's baby was considered "unadoptable." He would be kept until there was room in an institution.

He was born addicted to heroin. Some symptoms expected to resolve with withdrawal care. Some were to be permanent; digestive disorders, blind in one eye. Other damages including a curvature of the spine that was quite obvious.

He was pathetic. We were to have him longer and love him more. At the close of eight months, space in the institution was available.

He passed the physical!

He was adoptable!

With symptoms gone, both eyes bright and strong, spine straight as a baby's back…he was adopted.

Adopted by a naval family who knew his background. They saw him as a "sign and wonder."

We sent him with his family on to the Philippines.

Our going away gift was a Bible inscribed:

From those who loved you first,

Order of St. Luke, Wichita, Ks.

"The Holy Spirit is like a string that holds our necklace together, too."

And so it was, another expanded ministry on the way. The first baby showed clearly our specific gift was in healing prayer teams.

Then another gift, healing in dying, that kept us ever mindful of our vows even unto this day, and those yet to come.

Healing In Dying

Nina came to us for healing of cancer. Her husband waited in the car. We don't know what the conversation was when she went out later waving an application for OSL novitiate.

We seldom had a more vibrant and enthusiastic new member than Nina. The Healing Prayer Teams were her niche. She traveled with us, studied, joined conference teams. She was our center piece.

One night, years later, the hospital called. They had just admitted Nina for possible recurrence of the cancer.

Her teams surrounded her with loving concern as she expected. With her humor, she insisted.

The last to leave one night hesitated when Nina whispered for something.

She drew closer to Nina and asked her to repeat.

Nina whispered, "pizza."

"Pizza?"

"Pizza."

We could certainly arrange that!

"Yes," it was fine with floor supervision.

"No," there wasn't an oven. Fridge and sink, but no oven.

After group discussion with Nina the decision was made. She would like a pizza oven in the kitchen now. It would be her memorial from us.

And so it was. Complete with a memorial plaque.

Nina had her pizza, "at night when it's still, lonely and I'm hungry."

Some weeks later in her gentle soft voice she whispered, "It is good to help people live. It is good to help people die."

And so it was. She unfolded her hands and left us.

Nina's legacy?

"It is good to help people live.

It is good to help people die."

Christian Healing

Soon an Episcopal priest, Fr. Bob Layne, not only listened, but also invited me to his day off so "we could really talk." We did. For most of the day.

Then, he asked, "Would you be interested in teaching a class on healing for Lent?"

"Me?"

This was only fall. By Lent I had easily churned through two reams of paper, trying to discern the necessities needed for a one-hour class.

When it finally came, I sat in the seat indicated at the front of the room. Adrenalin spurting like alka-seltzer. I watched people pour in. A flash of panic whacked me! What if none of these people are interested in healing? Just the Priest? Do they even know? What will they do when I tell them? They're juggling coffee, donuts and chairs; about one-hundred. Would they stop rattling lap trays? Would they listen? Leave?

Affirmation was about to become a necessity. To my right a capable looking woman was erasing the chalkboard, adjusting the podium. I stepped up and introduced myself and asked if she thought there was an interest here in the subject of healing.

"Honey," she twanged. "These people come in here every Sunday morning and they listen to anything."

They were settling in now. Tables move. Chairs drag. Coffee splashes.

"Pass the donuts!"

"Over here, John."

"That's my seat."

It's Episcopal all right.

I honed in on a precious little man perched on a front row seat. Quiet. Smiling at me. I'll return to him again and again for affirmation.

I had been defining Christian healing. What is it?

"We believe it is the process of becoming whole. The power in that process is God. The activator of that power is prayer. Whether brokenness is in body, mind, spirit, relational or situational, healing is the process that reconciles these parts or combinations thereof to their original health or intention. Power may be processed through all medications, therapies, instruments or none. Our Lord uses them all, He still does and expects us too.

God wants us to be whole. When we are finally at-one-ment with Him, we will be complete...meanwhile we are all on our way in the process of becoming.

Who Are The Ministers?

We are. Christians are the mystical body of Christ. We are the physical channels of His Holy Spirit. We are no less diverse or motley than His first disciples. He still calls, trains, empowers and sends. Our responsibility is obedience. We are responsible for the use and development of His gifts to use for each other."

At the closure of my talk the little smiling man who had unknowingly encouraged me all the way came quickly to shake my hand and still smiling proclaimed,

"Do come again. I haven't the slightest idea what you're talking about but you sure seemed to."

And Then One Day

A national publication saw us as newsworthy; "Reverend Rufus Womble's induction of the largest chapter of the Order of St. Luke ever inducted in the United States at St. Christopher's Church, Wichita, Ks."

Following the article we were offered an invitation by the Vice Warden of OSL that I included in a letter to all the OSL members:

Order of St. Luke the Physician, International

Wichita Chapter Headquarters

St. Christopher's Church

2211 South Bluff

Greetings, in His Name!

And welcome into the most exciting of all seasons ever!

The usual ministries are from constant to flourishing. New ones are sprouting into full view and the autumn harvest, "with fruit are bending down."

Once upon a time last spring at Francis McNutt's Tulsa Workshop, Father Farr said to me, quite casually, over lunch, "I would like you to lead a workshop for the National Conference in Denver next October and, (tucking his napkin) the Wichita people to be prayer group leaders."

The mountain top happening I felt the rest of that day could be best described by Sue, who bumped into me round a corner, clamped onto my shoulders, and said face to face in popeyed wonder, "Who kissed you?"

"Next October," is here. We've received our assignment. The job is clear-cut. We are responsible for the second of twenty-four workshops. Our subject; "Developing The Healing Prayer Team." Every member, every person in the Order of St. Luke can feel and be part of this tremendous opportunity. Those who will not be there physically have perhaps the heaviest load – prayer support. Prayer that is the mightiest force in the Universe.

A part of Father Farr's charge to us:

"We trust you will be much in prayer concerning how the Lord would direct you in leading this important phase of the National Conference."

Thank you for being willing to be one of God's resources for the rich in blessings He will give us all. Thank you.

Gratefully,

Charles Albert Farr

Vice Warden, O.S.L., Conference Host

Our Lord's charge to us?

"Pray for one another that you may be healed."

Our obligation? Obedience.

Agape,

Virginia

(Virginia Winters, Chapter Convener)

Through the Order of St. Luke The Physician, I had learned that the power of the Holy Spirit through one person was magnified through the ministry of the group in healing prayer teams. "For where two or three have gathered together in My name, there I am in their midst."[5]

Yet there was still more to learn.
Much More.

---

[5] Matthew 18:20

"Things I Have Told You"

About Intercession

About

Intercession

To discern the nature of intercession and a process that will take us there is the desire of this chapter.

First, the process, which is this: Experience is showing, instruction is telling and combining is knowing; Knowing that is insight, sync of heart and mind.

It becomes your truth.

Part I: Experience.

Journal entry of numinous dream; a Night Journey.

Part II: Reflection.

Combining experience and reflection taught a truth.

The chapter closes with a reflective teaching and reminds the reader that if prayer is our deepest communion with Him then we should certainly be able to discern the expressible truths therein,

so we begin to learn…

About

Intercession

Night Journey

"Prayer is the mightiest force in the universe."[6] It comes forth as we commune with Him, with our desire to join Him, to co-create with Him, to be with Him in that same force that heals shame, penetrates matter, and creates the atom: the same force. When you stand before the Father and offer yourself with Christ for my wholeness, that is intercessory prayer. To discern the nature of intercession and a process that will take us there is the desire of this story. First, the process.

It's actually quite a simple process, one that brought understanding to me. Perhaps it will hold a truth for you, too. It is this: instruction is telling, experience is showing and combining the instruction and the experience is knowing--knowing that is insight, sync of mind and heart. It becomes your truth. Here is an example of an experience that recalled a teaching.

In prayer group a few years ago, I heard myself say, "Thank you for the privilege of prayer."

Privilege? Prayer? Prayer is need, desire, ought, should, can, and so on, but privilege? He was, I knew, in me, above me. He breathed life in me. He birthed the

---

[6] Frank Laubach, *Prayer, The Mightiest Force in the World*, Fleming H. Revell Co

idea of me. And just today being with Him in prayer became privilege.

June, standing beside me, brightened, "Privilege? Hadn't thought of that. It is, isn't it?"

"IT IS!"

The insight shot around the room like popcorn. Suddenly prayer had a new dimension for us. A new truth. Prayer is indeed a privilege.

And now, the teaching of long ago recalled.

Last night, listening to the radio what do you suppose I heard? The hymn, a theme of my childhood, the first song I played on the piano...

> What a friend we have in Jesus
>
> All our sins and griefs to bear
>
> *What a privilege to carry*
>
> Everything to God in prayer.

There it was. A childhood time of telling, and finally, joining the experience: the knowing. A truth. Experience and instruction do not come in sequential order. Sometimes the instruction, the teaching, is best understood later on - perhaps catching up to an experience that calls forth the AHA! Or, maybe, experience lies brooding or dormant till the teaching comes. And now, that same process into a deeper discernment of the nature of intercession, beginning with the experience.

Night Journey

The Experience

Part I

Night Journey

The Experience

Bedtime was as usual. Same time. Same bed. Same kind of day as yesterday, and the day before. Nothing in my life situation, or conscious awareness, to suggest anything other than the usual night's sleep ahead; certainly not the night it came to be.

Journal

Sometime after falling asleep, I found myself drifting through the night. I was moving west, leaving the coast of the United States. I was high enough that looking down I could see the outline of all the west coast, part of Mexico, and part of Canada. But the United States--the west coast of the United States was in the center. This was focused. And I could see the rugged coastline and the whitecaps lunging toward the beaches, frothing and fuming, and the deep colors of blues and greens in the ocean beneath me, and it was bright day. I could see the horizon all around, and I was moving straight west. I was in awe of the beauty of the coast of our country, the colors in the sea, the blues in the sky, the softness of the air and the cleanness, the purity, the freedom, just moving, just being a part of and moving in this silent space. The coastline began to fade from view and in a while the east was all horizon, as was all around me, as far as there was, to the edges of the earth. The beautiful ocean groaning and resting and living and churning and beautiful. I moved silently west.

In a little while, out of the southwest, a plane came into view. It was an American plane, a war plane; it was coming out of the war zone. There were two pilots, and the plane was in trouble. I sensed the fear in the crew and wondered if they were going to make it to the coast. I was curious about them and just what their trouble might be so I moved toward them. I came near enough to see the anxiety on their faces and their doing various things with the instrument panels. Just the instant I was aware of this, the sputtering and fuming stopped. The plane again came into their control and was moving steadily toward the coast of America, as it was supposed to. They tossed their heads back and they were smiling and happy and all was okay. And so I watched them move on east, and I went on with my journey.

I was now moving north and west. I was beginning to know a sense of mission. I didn't know what that might be, except that it was something I was going to do, because I was supposed to and something that I wanted to do. There wasn't any question about it. I was just going. I was enjoying the sensation of freedom, the joy in that good feeling in service...service without responsibility for it.

In a while, I began to move down into a little lower altitude and realized that I was going in on, focusing in on, where I was supposed to be going. It seemed to me it was Russia. It was a cold country.

It was sundown. I suppose the sun had just barely dipped because there was that evening glow of light without color. Yes, that was it - light, but not like sunlight. Then, I saw exactly where I was supposed to go. I was moving toward a four-plex. It was built on a long east to west lot facing north. There was a street on the north and one on the east. Along the northern front of the four-plex was a sidewalk that ran the length of it all. Then, in front of each apartment was a little jut of sidewalk out to the main walk. There was probably two or three feet of snow on the ground. The yard was elevated so that in grass season, one would have to mow at an angle for about two feet. But now, the snow was deep. I moved down toward the sidewalk along the north of the four-plex. I could see that someone had swept it clean. There was just a little sifting fresh snow on the walk brushed with broom marks. It was still light enough to see as I approached. Still enough glow to twinkle the snow.

There was a little boy, I suppose four or five years old, standing there, bundled in a snow suit - a little woolly earth colored snowsuit. He looked up toward me, and I was delighted by his bright little face. His cheeks were pink, eyes glowing and the little nose dripping. I thought, "What a dear, dear child..." And then, I had a sudden startle because he was looking straight at me and I thought, " Oh, my, I don't want to frighten him," and at the same thought I knew he couldn't see me, anyway. Or, could he?

I looked on past the little boy because my destination was the four-plex on the west end - the furthest one down.

I went inside. The apartment was the usual square floor plan so that the door opens into the living room that faces north. Most of the living room was to my right at the door. The kitchen/eating area was on the south end of that room. To my left was the other side of the square, two bedrooms and bath. I moved from the front door in the living room to the northwest corner of that ceiling. I looked toward the kitchen end.

There was a man standing there with two little boys. They were maybe five and seven years old. I had the impression that the man was a young widower. He was medium height, with neat black, oiled hair. He wore a black leather jacket, hip length, black shoes and long cared for heavy work shoes. I also had the impression that he drove some kind of public utility vehicle. He was employed by the city as a driver of some sort.

The kids. Their hair was thick and tangled. They were as dirty as their misfit clothes. The babysitter had left, and he was just home from work.

The house was a shambles...a mess. Food spilled on the floor, newspapers and stuff scattered the living room. Where they had eaten breakfast, on the table, cereal was still in the dishes, dried in the milk. He just stood there between the boys, stooped, arms dangling, wanting to cry. Feelings about his wife were churning in him. "Why did you leave me? Why did you have to die on me and leave me in this hopeless mess?" And then, the surge of guilt, "These poor kids - don't have a mother, and I'm sorry for myself." He was wallowing in a mixture of guilt, confusion, and anger. He was clinching his fists and his eyes, gritting his teeth in surges of rage.

I watched him, knew him and loved him. I felt such compassion for him surge through me, well up in me, that for a moment, I *was* compassion! Then I moved into the swirl of another Spirit moving from the ceiling down toward him and into him. Together, we engulfed him with love. We moved around him and through him, above him and in front of him, behind him. We permeated him with Love.

When it was time to move away, I backed into the ceiling again and observed him. He began to straighten his shoulders a bit. He unclenched his hands, then his face. He took a couple of deep breaths. A touch of a smile came to his mouth. He took hold of a little boy's hand on each side of him. He said,

"Well, fellas, then looking down at them, "Let's get with it...let's clean this mess up. Here."

And he grabbed sacks from under the sink for each child and they all began to laugh and romp around with each other, all the while stuffing the sacks with whatever was on the floor nearest them.

I enjoyed them for awhile and when I left, there was joy and laughter and love in that place and in those hearts.

My next recollection was of sitting on the side of my bed, holding my breath in the wonder of it. A voice in my heart said, "This is how you are used in prayer."

What is this? The mystery. The awe. There *is* a sound in silence...humming. How to hold onto this?

Make it tangible. Write it down. Never let it go.

I nearly missed the purpose of it all "This is how you are used in prayer."

What did that mean? Just the sound of it seemed to interrupt the journey. But remembering that not listening to what He tells me or not paying attention to what He shows me has been the root of most of my undoing, I journaled what seemed to be an appendage; it has since encouraged me deeper into the growing pains of prayer. Later, in that day I decided I should also include another probable aside...that airplane. It was unnecessary. Or was it?

The experience seemed to lay dormant for a few years until I realized bits and pieces had come to mind from time to time: a flash of the view, a question about compassion, or why is blue? Being a perennial design seeker, I began to pay attention. Before long it was obvious the remembrances came when I was in prayer - or in the study, teaching, or wondering about prayer. As I became more aware of the teaching out of the experience of the "night journey" I deliberately pursued it.

"What are you saying to me about that, Lord?" or "I hear the story, but what else does it mean?"

For instance, I have three sons for whom I pray without ceasing. The eldest, Randy, came to mind on a flight I was taking from Wichita to Orlando, Florida. We were somewhere above the clouds; you know the view - a bed of billows covering the world. The whole world is white and still. I remember wondering how could God personally love every single person in such vastness? How is that possible?

Then, He asked, "How can you love Randy from here to California?"

"What difference does that make? *Where* he is has nothing to do with it," I answered.

He said to me, "Right! Time and space are unbounded. Love knows it is free."

So, love is immeasurable. What IS the distance between me in Orlando, Randy in Los Angeles, and the man in Russia? None.

In the quiet after the exchange, I prayed for Randy,

"Lord, I have no idea what's going on in Randy's life right now - where he is or how he is, so hold him close, keep him in your Presence."

About two weeks later, a rarity came in the form of a letter from Randy. After chit-chat and updates, he told of a "strange experience a couple of weeks ago." It seems that just before boarding a flight, he had a hunch not to. He is a frequent flyer and this is not usual. He wrote:

> "...hunches like this a couple or three times a year. No problem. Just take next flight. However, this would have caused some real inconvenience to those meeting me. I got on reluctantly. I was a bit uneasy all the way to Denver, but everything was fine...DID miss my connecting flight and

had one of those layovers. Thought about you a lot. Nothing special. Just thinking.

I *do* hope you're sitting down.

Are you?

The flight I missed exploded on landing in Dallas."

Another time, our second son, Dennis, was in Viet Nam - a place called Da Nang. That's all I knew. I asked the Lord to surround him, hold him in His light all the time there and all the way home. The image I saw was of him walking inside an aura of bright light, that clung to his body in every motion. Twice a day I held this image in prayer. Morning and night. I saw him in this cocoon of protection.

The year he was on the "front line" in Da Nang - if, indeed such a line could be defined in that war - one of his duties was the night mail. He drove the mail truck with its lights out to a specific spot on the runway, deposited the mail bags, and screeched out of the way for the incoming, blacked out pick-up plane. He had an exact minute to enter and leave the runway, IN THE DARK. Timing was all...He wrote:

"...Last night's run was a...well, I dunno...started out as usual. Same routine, out to the runway, unload the bags, hop in the truck and "home." Last night, it went like that till "hop in the truck." It died. Dead as a mackerel. Jumped out, did all I knew, felt cables and stuff. I wanted to run. Then I heard the plane. I couldn't. He wouldn't know. I was absolutely helpless. I knew it. I prayed. Stood there. Then, kinda like automatic, I reached back under the hood, did something, slammed it, hopped back in. It STARTED! Somehow I was back in the mailroom, plane and bags were gone, runway still. I thank the Lord, Mom; I thank Him."

To this day, every day, in prayers for my family, Dennis (he's now with wife and three children) is in the same aura of light, striding at his usual pace.

In the two preceding experiences, both boys were far away physically. So, what did I do right for them? Well, actually, not much. I simply offered them to God and left them with Him. I suspect submission to His choices was not because I thought it was the right thing to do but because I could do nothing ELSE. I didn't KNOW anything else to do. Like the man who pleaded for help at midnight,[7] I was impotent, empty. Because of my emptiness there was room for Him. Had I been where the boys were physically at these times I, no doubt, would have given the Lord directions day and night, right and left.

---

[7] Luke 11:5-8

It's different for Sam, our youngest, who may or may not be as fortunate as his brothers, depending on your point of view. He lives in the same town with us. His business is in the same building as ours. It isn't that I don't pray God's will be done in his life; it's just that I have access to much reason for advice and counsel for the Lord - on the chance He doesn't see as close up as I, or, He's out in the Garden someplace and misses an important point.

Of course, I say this with tongue-in-cheek. The temptation to instruct God, to BE God, is ever in us. Most of the time I seem to be able to let God be God with special intention only, and or, because I don't see over the fence. I have learned to yield to His will, finally... repeatedly. Sometimes. Once in a while.

How does one learn to submit to Him more often? By asking. Teach me. Teach me to pray. For instance, where *is* the place of petition in intercession?

"You have not because you ask not" and then, "You have not because you pray amiss." [8]

Teach me about "Amiss."

See the cycle?

Learning ends with questions, doesn't it?

Teach me

In the night

I'll remember

In the light.

---

[8] James 4:3

Night Journey

Reflection

Part II

Reflection

In the days to follow I spent long hours savoring Dennis' letter, meditating on the meanings in both journeys, and thanking the Lord for the things he has told me beyond what I know, beneath what I will know. I am content on this plateau resting in the reflections that in due season, will impel me to the next.

I share some of these reflections that they may be, or become, a part of your truth. (In no sense do I offer them as "how-to's" because I believe Love transcends techniques, even the best ones.)

One reflection that kept sifting back into first place was the necessity to:

1) Commit:

To commit is to say "yes" to His request to intercede. He calls us constantly; we respond constantly, one way or another.

After we have made that commitment, we...

2) Enter:

To wait for the touch of His Grace, the signal to begin.

Then go with Him in that flow. Stay in the motion of grace. Abiding has begun. Your spirit begins to emerge from self into His. We are becoming one with the Great Intercessor.

"He that is joined with the Lord is one spirit." [9]
As we join we begin to...

3) Abandon:

I offer all that I am, self, gifts, spirit and will, ALL in utter abandonment to Him for His use of me. It is our abandonment of self for His use, our abiding in each other, that enfolds us into His Love. His is the Love that heals, that enhances, infuses ours. It is in flowing toward the center of His Love that my will evaporates, our woundedness recognizes itself and we...

4) Identify:

To know, to feel with, the recipient is to identify. Our own woundedness is redeemable, it has become transformed in His Love. To "bear one another's burdens that you may be healed" is to come together inside His love for His transforming. So, that we may...

5) Rejoice!:

In true intercession we have become one with Him, the Physician, the great intercessor. [10] Imagine the outpouring if each of us would stand in the gap, offering, listening, responding, without concern with the outcome? Imagine trusting Him like that. To offer all that we are for His use...no advice, instructions,

---

[9] I Corinthians 6:17
[10] John 17

directions, explanations, just sheer abandonment in His service. Can you stand there and risk misunderstanding? Or, worse; understanding? Can you release that, too?

REJOICE!

"For we are members of His body, His flesh and bones."[11] "Now you are the body of Christ and members in particular."[12] *We are the mystical body and physical instrument of Christ on earth.*

If, we believe this, Andrew Murray contends,

"Intercession will become the first thing we take refuge in when we seek Blessing for others. And the very last thing for which we cannot find time."

He blesses us through prayers for each other. Paul Cho tells us,[13]

"Intercessory prayer is necessary in the fulfillment of God's divine will. This does NOT mean God is incapable of bringing His will to pass but He has CHOSEN to include us in the realization of His will. Therefore, those who enter a ministry of intercession actually become an integral part of God's plan and purpose."

And, so the "mightiest force" *is* available. The experience of that force in intercession differs from other prayer forms in that we are willing to be a part of the solution, to be used as a gift for the other. For the life of the world. There is a process revealed, according to our need to know, through Jesus Christ, the teacher.

---

[11] I Corinthians 6:15
[12] I Corinthians 12:27
[13] Paul Yonggi Cho, pastor of the Full Gospel Central Church in Seoul, Korea.

Do you want your life to make a difference? That your time has made a place in the scheme of things? Be an intercessor...Choose to be with Him in prayer. When you allow God the Father, through His Son, in His Spirit to come through and in you to love one another, your life has changed the world.

"Things I Have Told You"

About Weavers

About

Weavers

All of our days before this one are the prelude for the years to come.

This is one of the very special gifts for the autumn of life. Spring and summer have special gifts too, but they are a prologue to gifts kept especially for autumn.

Those of you in spring and summer seasons may be looking a bit thoughtful. Those in autumn of life are smiling with me.

One gift that we have not known clearly in the spring and summer seasons of our lives is retrospect. In the autumn we can see our journey now from mountain tops, valleys, through the plateaus and deserts; we see all the shoulds and the aughts, some that didn't matter anyway. We see an overview of death into life, through the glass a little bit more clearly.

Autumn is the one season that prepares us for the winter of rest that precedes a new spring, the ultimate healing.

I recalled a legend. And like most "true" legends it begins with, "Once upon a time . . ."

There was a man thrown into a dungeon
for life and for a crime he did not commit.
The only light came through the iron gate.
Inside the dungeon were a metal bed and a

commode. That was all. He saw no one except for the guard who brought food once a day.

His wife was allowed to come at rare and specific times, but only to speak with him briefly. They could not touch. They were caught once hugging through the bars. Visits were moved farther away and for shorter times.

One day she went to see the captain of the guards. She was very concerned about her husband's knees. He spent most of his time kneeling in prayer and they were torn and bleeding. She asked if she could bring her husband a small rug for kneeling. She persisted and finally the captain relented and said, "Well, all right. But bring it to me. You cannot hand it through the bars to him yourself."

Weeks later she came in with the rug she had made for him. The guards looked it over and decided she was smuggling nothing. So they gave it to him.

He began to kneel on the rug for his prayers. His knees began to heal and the bleeding stopped.

In a few weeks, when the guards were making their regular rounds, the iron gate was open. He was gone.

His wife had been able to slowly but surely make an imprint of the keyhole when they had hugged that day, and she had woven the design into the rug. He knew what to look for.

He had, over a very long time, taken little bits of metal out of the bed and the commode, and made the key.

A new life came out of the dying one, because he had looked for a design he knew would be there from the one he loved and trusted. Are you looking for the design your Weaver has made for you?

"Things I Have Told You"

About Spiritual Direction

Discerning Your Journey

Discerning your journey by paying attention to its design.

Finding spiritual direction revealed in the weaving of experiences in healing of body, mind, human spirit and Holy Spirit over and in all.

About
Spiritual Direction

Spiritual direction is an art form.

Spiritual direction heals, because the spirit of the law
transcends the letter of the law.

Spiritual direction heals, because

love transcends techniques.

Listening with love feeds

the empty broken spirit

in each of us.

About

Spiritual Direction

Spiritual Director

It was a cozy fireside night in late September, decades ago. Just right for cruising scriptures, pausing on a page or two then another. Ahh, yes, Samuel. One of my favorites. Read. Then, read again: I Samuel: 1-20.

> "Now, the boy Samuel was serving Yahweh in the presence of Eli; In those days it was rare for Yahweh to speak; visions were uncommon.
>
> One day, it happened that Eli was lying down in his room. His eyes were beginning to grow dim; he could no longer see.
>
> The lamp of God had not yet gone out and Samuel was lying in Yahweh's sanctuary where the Ark of God was, when Yahweh calls, "Samuel! Samuel!"
>
> He answered, "Here I am," and running to Eli, he said,
>
> "Here I am, as you called me."

Eli said, " I did not call. Go back and lie down."

So he went and lay down, and again Yahweh called, "Samuel! Samuel!"

He got up and went to Eli and said, "Here I am as you called me."

He replied, "I did not call, my son; go back and lie down." As yet, Samuel had no knowledge of Yahweh.

And the word of Yahweh had not yet been revealed to him.

Again, Yahweh called the third time. He got up and went to Eli and said,

"Here I am as you called me."

Eli then understood that Yahweh was calling the child, and he said to Samuel, "Go and lie down, and if someone calls say, "Speak, Yahweh; for your servant is listening."

So Samuel went and lay down in his place.

Yahweh then came and stood by, calling as he had done before, "Samuel!" "Samuel!"

Samuel answered, "Speak Yahweh for your servant is listening."

Eli pointed Samuel toward *the* Director, God himself. Eli was a good Director: loved, listened, paid attention to Samuel. Eli was honest with Samuel. Eli was Samuel's spiritual director. Yahweh was the ultimate Director for both.

He listened and then directed him to *the* Director, who is God.

He did not say, "Just a minute Samuel. I'll check it out for you, speak to the Director and get back with you."

Or, "No problem. Anything else you want me to ask for you?"

No. Eli was not the source of answers. He knew who was. Samuel did not question or hesitate. He trusted the wisdom of Eli.

Pondering the story I patted my abdomen. I was carrying my third child. A boy would be called Samuel.

The baby was a boy.

His name is Samuel.

He is Samuel.

Spiritual Direction

I was not aware the design in my kneeler was showing me what would become the ultimate ministry of my life; spiritual direction. All other teachings were stepping stones. I didn't even know what it was till the chaplain told me that I just did. It was the woman in room number 522.

A Hospital Story

Unforgettable memories are sometimes understood in retrospect. It was for me in the closure of hospital Pastoral Care training into the beginning of its practice. My certification read: "Pastoral Care in Living and Dying." This is good.

I knelt alone in the chapel, clutching my first-rounds card. Praying our usual closing prayer for the first time without a chaplain. We always prayed together: "Let me be an instrument of your healing love and let someone see you in me today."

Unexpectedly I added, "Help me meet the people where they are and go with them where they need to be with you. Amen."

The addition was the whispered beginning of my call to spiritual direction.

It was Monday. My first patient was an elderly woman.

When I said "Good Morning" she squinted up at me and said, "Virginia! I knew you would come. Where have you been?!"

(Who is this woman? Where do I know her from?)

"Now, where do you think I've been?"

She hesitated then questioned, "Grocery store?"

"Right." Long silence.

"How did Bruce do on his tests?"

"About as usual," I answered. She did not know me.

"I'm sure he was the best. He's the smartest of the three don't you think?" she asked.

"Yes. He was the best. We expected it too."

"Did I get any mail?"

"I'll check and see."

We kept this up a while. She dozed off. I prayed quietly and left.

On Tuesday, she was animated and quite talkative…wandering through her life. Sometimes apparently talking to no one in particular, sometimes looking at me a little surprised and confused. She wanted to talk about forgiveness.

In a while, she was able to share with me through tears, stops and starts about her experience with incest. She looked at me, then as if for the first time and said distinctly, "I've never said that out loud in my life!"

We went through the process of forgiveness together.

After a time of quiet and rest, she turned to me with the same expression as yesterday, "Remember our prayer together when you were a little girl?"

I said, "How could I forget?"

"Let's pray together again." She smiles.

"All right. You begin," I suggested slowly.

It was easy; "Now I lay me down to sleep. I pray the Lord my soul to keep. If I should die before I wake, I pray the Lord my soul to take."

We made it. She closed her eyes. I tucked her in, kissed her forehead, and backed out of the room.

Tomorrow perhaps I would learn who she thought I was.

On Wednesday, day three, I walked in to find her bed empty. She had died in her sleep.

("If I should die before I wake.") I learned, her confusion that Monday was because she didn't know that her daughter had been in a car wreck Saturday night. She died Sunday. I came on Monday.

Her daughter's name? Virginia...of course.

The chaplain asked how long I'd had interest in spiritual direction.

"What's that?"

"What you just did."

Years later the essence of spiritual direction is still; "Lord, help me to meet the people where they are and go with them where they need to be with you."

The same week a newspaper article announced a presentation on Spiritual Direction in a nearby health center that weekend. I was the first one there.

What is this? I was spellbound with the subject and the presenter.

We talked quite a bit overtime after and I asked if we could pursue the subject tomorrow?

Well, no, he was leaving late afternoon the next day. I lived close to where he was staying and sure, he'd try to work in an hour or so. And he did.

As a matter of fact he was early. I invited him in the kitchen where I was finishing up some preparations for a dinner party that night. He helped with things like,

"Can you reach the vanilla – right behind you - second shelf?"

"Sure."

We squished in some memorable time and teaching till we finished in the kitchen.

I was so inspired till a mid-week jolt. An invitation and summer schedule for Pecos, Benedictine Abbey, New Mexico on Spiritual Direction arrived in the mail. The picture on the brochure was who?

Morton Kelsey.

Morton Kelsey! Ye Pete! And I asked *him* to pass the vanilla?

The design in my kneeler had led into amazing grace.

Pecos Benedictine Abbey became home base for the study of Spiritual Direction. When the first term was closing, the auditorium clearing, he and I were sitting alone on the stage, feet dangling, to peruse the session. My journal reads: "We do this often-sit on the stage floor and talk. Today, as usual he gets so quickly, concisely to the point."

My last question to him was, "With all the new methods, we can instant check, almost any part of us...stop at a lab and wait a minute...go to the grocery for a blood-pressure check...the mall offers instant cholesterol checks...a few minutes with the MBTI[14], and you instantly know how best to function. You'll uncover your weaknesses and strengths, even the most

---

[14] Isabel Briggs Myers, Myers-Briggs Type Indicator (MBTI), *Gifts Differing: Understanding Personality Type,* Davies-Black Publishing.

effective prayer model for you. Wouldn't it be neat if we could get an instant soul check? Like, how healthy is my spirituality? Poke in a card to get a scale in colored blinks?"

He said, "Much simpler than that m'dear. Just a simple question."

"Really?"

"What question?"

"Do you love more? More than you did?"

"How much do you love?"

Hmmm...

Healing Through Spiritual Direction

The study and practice of spiritual direction became, and still is the ministry of my life – the Weaver showed me.

Spiritual direction is not new: revival is for us. God has regularly stirred His people into a gnawing hunger for intimacy with Him, to feed on rootedness in Him, to stop nibbling leaves.

Spiritual direction heals because it restores, reconciles and facilitates our walk with God. It can support, connect, go through, all other ministries.

Spiritual direction heals because the spirit of the Law transcends the letter of the Law.

Spiritual direction heals because love transcends techniques. To stay quiet and listen to your soul throb and release into clarification is assertive surrender.

Spiritual direction is an art form, a gift, a charism, that needs training and supervision but never at exclusion of the creative freedom of the Holy Spirit.

The essence of spiritual direction is in discerning the motion of the Holy Spirit's presence: God's presence and yours to each other.

Henry Nouwen in his book, *Creative Ministry*, states, "Healing ministries call for creative weakness. In our weakness is God's strength known."

In spiritual direction knowing the basics provides only the launching pad and that's all I *need* to know. To go *with* because I don't know. To *stay with* because neither of us knows.

To rejoice together in the Emmaus journey's "Aha!"

That *is* the "creative weakness" that gives ministry its momentum!"

'Tis human fortunes
Happiest height to be
A spirit melodious, lucid,
Poised and Whole.
Second, in order
Of felicity is to
Walk with
Such a soul.

I am.
Sometimes.
I do.
A lot.

"Things I Have Told You"

⤳ About Deserts ⤲

About

Deserts

"He found Him in a desert land, and in the howling waste of the wilderness."[15]

Jesus went into the desert from Jordon to prepare for the rest of His ministry.

Jesus was able to meet temptation, fight off the evil, sweat through anguish, individuation of His humanity, because He knew going into the desert He was God's beloved, a love that would go with Him all the way. Always. Through deserts of struggle or rest. He knew His identity was in God. He knew His ministry was His Father's and in His life and power.

"I'll do what I see my Father do."

His preparation for ministry to come was complete. The prelude to Jesus' ministry had ended. Journeying the desert is to be with God and in the doing meet our selves, and like Jesus, discover our own identity...to know who we are.

Any desert, of painful body, broken spirit, confused mind, desert of heart can be long stretch of silence or howling waste of wilderness.

We too, find God in our deserts, as have all great religions in the world found theirs. He is more

---

[15] Deuteronomy 31:30

discernable there. In that struggle we discover our own identity.

On a recent pilgrimage to the Holy Land, I literally stood there in Jesus' desert. It is bleak, colorless, jagged ridges, deep gorges, slate, rock and stubble stretched to the horizon in haunting stillness.

Loneliness. Stretches of silent sand. I walked a while myself. He prepared and gifted me with a new facet of ministry.

In darkness it's easier to catch a spark of God's light slowly coming to full view, like one star in the night sky. In morning light I wandered on down to Galilee. I was there. On the spot. In Galilee. I stood, eyes closed as in a time capsule. The morning crunch of the gathering crowd brought hope, doubt, faith, fear...swirls of dust. Stench of sick. Power of Love was mounting, waiting. Waiting for Jesus...this morning... He was coming.

Imaging Jesus with fishermen, my right foot stumbled on a rock. A rock pointing downward to the sea. I brought it home. It rests on my prayer table pointing to the cross.

Tiberius At Dawn

There have been dawns in other lands,

That came

With banners flung across the sea;

There have been skies of blended pearl of flame

But this is spring and dawn and Galilee!

In these grave hours

When the master's heart

Ached with bitter sorrows men have known,

Perhaps they slept, while he walked apart,

And braved the beauty of this dawn, alone.

Again there is a presence on the sea

The Master walks at dawn by Galilee.

Mary Brant Whiteside

Healing, defined, as the process of becoming whole in God, has never changed. God only knows how much we try to change it.

Since the beginning, healing has been in reconciling the parts in us, with other, in the permeating love of an unlimited God. Terminology changes. Now "holistic" is the term.

That we are all on our way…we are all wounded healers.

Poustinia

Back home from the Holy Land, and as usual reveling in browsing a bookstore till a specific book spoke to me. Especially, on a dreary rainy Saturday afternoon, snuggling into the evening to come. And there it was.

In the wall by the fireplace, one said, "Here. Here I am." It was titled, "Poustinia;" "The Russian word for hermitage or a desert place to meet and be with God alone." Like Jesus' desert; to be alone with God. No interference; just silence and privacy.

OSL gathered for retreat once a month. We met in a guesthouse on a nearby lake. Lake Santa Fe. How about some time spent being more specific, more descriptive? A time more intentional for personal spiritual growth. More silence. More aloneness down the dirt paths along the lakeside. More introspection. More personal, private space with our Lord. Closure time sharing thoughts or quietly tucking our experience in to take away. Freedom either way.

And so began our journey with Poustinia in the country. Retreats for OSL and friends. A fruitful year later it ended as abruptly as it started. A death in the family meant selling the property and sorrow all the way around. Much life had been given. Much would be lost. Or would it?

My husband and I moved to Midtown Wichita on the second floor of a two-story building belonging to our family; it had been apartments for World War II workers. It emptied after the war ended. It just stood there. Dwight had a great idea. Why not remodel the upstairs for us? Why not? And so it was.

He was never happier than when he had a hammer and saw, lots of boards, walls to tear down and creative beauty came forth. We loved 'junkin,' finding antiques and restoring. What better place than a new-old building?

It was beautiful indeed. Just right for us. He built me a lovely library room that was cozy and drenched in hospitality.

Some continued to come for spiritual direction. Some to begin. Others for closure.

Ahh! Poustinia upstairs!

Affirmations seem to swirl slowly in and around us. None more treasured than a visit from my Bishop... Bishop Smalley.[16] It was a most joyful intimate time of sharing stories and faith, and the affirmation on, "Your good and important ministry."

So special to me was his gift to Poustinia library. Even my Bishop shared Poustinia. Such affirmation peaked this blessed time.

Meanwhile I was invited to the See Christ Retreat Groups with the Acuto Center in Newman College. Out of the country Poustinia came many new and abiding friendships. We hooked into each other wherever we were. Conference, workshops, coffee hours, and lunches for catch-up.

Even though scattered we never felt separated because we weren't.

The really big question came again? Poustinia was out of room.

Where else?

"How about the closed off downstairs?" Dwight asked.

"Are you kidding?" I responded.

"No!"

---

[16] I later asked permission to quote him. He chuckled and said, "Please do."

That was Dwight again. He was in his element and so was I. Get out the tools and shop for more old lights to hang. Wahoo!

There was plenty of room for the country group and then some. Through the new accommodations in the building transformation, came also the potential growth of staff which eventually grew to two chaplains, deacons, three spiritual directors, three counselors, a psychologist, etc, and the best of all, embracing five denominations.

Voila! Poustinia in the Marketplace, a Center for the Healing of Persons.

I was working on a brochure when Richard Foster called, "What are you doing down there? What's going on?"

I explained and he responded. We decided he should come down, give me some 'sound instructions' next Thursday.

"In the meantime," he announced, "Give 'em Heaven!"

I should have had a camera ready when he came in Thursday and stopped just inside the entrance by a stunning blue-framed piece on the wall:

To Poustinia

Give 'em Heaven!

Richard Foster

I hung our vision statement beneath it:

The Vision

In Poustinia we will journey toward
Wholeness inside God's Love; We will
Carry the radiance of His Holy Spirit
Into the Marketplace
Where other travelers will know and ask,
"Where did you meet the healing Christ today?
And you will answer,
"Over there…in Poustinia."

Fish & Chairs[17]

"We have nothing to give but five loaves and two fish."[18]

Summer is closing down and Poustinia In The Marketplace is still unfolding, as in 'flower.' The work has been truly blessed. And now three new directors and two more rooms are coming forth in expanding ministry. We have unfurnished space and heartfelt commitment. That's about it; half a loaf and one fish...except maybe for Mother's chairs.

She bought them when I was a child with the announcement, "These are for company." They were first displayed in the living room. The president of the Parents and Teachers chose the rocker: Mother, the straight back. The preacher the straight and Mother, the rocker. Dad smiled at Mother from the rocker, Mother nodded appreciation from the straight back.

I saw her rock my little brother to sleep, my cousin through fever, and a night watch with me through pneumonia. Then there were the nights I caught her nodding under the clock that tolled my curfew. She would re-do the chairs in spring, cover them for summer canning and freshen paint or covers for comfy winters. My childhood saw them in every room in the house at one time or another, And, finally, her indoor garden and sunroom.

---

[17] Fish & Chairs, Virginia M. Winters, Published 1994, Connections Magazine
[18] Matthew 14:17, American Standard Bible

When she died I brought them to my house and, of course, painted and recovered them for their place in the downstairs hall. Now, a few years later, and just one more time, they're getting a new coat. (taupe as the woodwork), and new covers (navy stripped ticking) for their new place in Poustinia.

Mother seemed near as I sanded, painted and remembered yesterday, How many times? How many colors? Remember the Victorian year? You painted them lush burgundy with tapestry covers in assorted shades of roses. Gorgeous transformation! But, then, you knew a lot about transformation, didn't you? I sense your usual excitement in being a part of the good things in my life. Welcome to Poustinia, Mother!

I thought about having them blessed, but aren't they? Prayers of thanksgiving are more in order. Or, offering...that's it...offering for His feeding includes it all. So, here they are, Lord, these chairs for your ministry. They are at *least* five loaves and two fishes.

A few people at the next Spiritual Directors International conference greeted me with, "How did the "Chairs" come out? How did the chair story end?"

It's a good thing they asked. I was looking for somebody else to tell.

To expand our group ministry we had added a new room that had emptied the cookie jar just short of any furnishings, except for Mother's wicker chairs waiting down the hall.

And so it was.

Slowly, assorted pieces gathered around the chairs, some folding, some straight backed, and even a sofa faced a larger circle, always focused toward the leadership of *the* chairs. Even when swivel rockers entered the scene, the first choice was where the feeding began,…in Mother's chairs.

Eventually, the motion of the Spirit seemed to be wending a new way in Poustinia. The Growth Groups (We don't call them support groups. Support implies holding up. Our groups get up and grow.) were becoming interested in including workshops for specific studies. Although an exciting turn of events, we found ourselves, again, short of space, teaching tools and funds.

We've maintained from the beginning that our first priority is ministry. Our second is pay for it. The first priority is always a cinch. The second wavers a lot. So, it seemed a reasonable alternative to checking out funding possibilities with an old friend, who was an experienced pro on both sides of the funding picture. We decided to talk it through from all directions, pray together, offered to the Lord and follow His guidance.

After a week or so of intentional prayer together…nothing. Then we decided to 'pray without ceasing,' to hold the issue before Him consistently.

One morning, a first directee, who always contributed fresh baked bread, brought twice the usual amount. The second directee, who always leaves a twenty-dollar bill folded in the Gift Box, left three. At closing time, another had left a check for two thousand dollars.

What more can He say?

We thought so too...with much praise and thanksgiving.

We should have been settled in by now with adequate space for private session groups, and small classes. Not so. We noted another motion of the Spirit that had been moving about quietly, subliminally.

For you to see this too you need to know that we see ministry as a team effort for the healing of body, mind, spirit by Holy Spirit. People have choices of one or the other or all. Also, down the block and around the corner is a place called The Center for Natural Healing Arts and Sciences. The owner is our son, Sam. This accounted for an occasional new directee's opening statement,

"Sam referred me to you. He says you're a good director."

I assure you it was reciprocal. Sam had a remarkable gift for healing body memories. A quite unexpected link began.

We were delightfully surprised to realize just how much we overlapped, how often we referred to each other, or should have, and decided from here on it would be intentional. Now you see it: all three. Body, mind and spirit slowly circling together into one.

And so, Poustinia glows with yet another facet. The chairs are adamant about their place in the group room, even though inundated with people and things now.

There's a long hallway centering Poustinia.

The chairs used to sit down there waiting in the shadows of a heavy fire door separating us from an old warehouse room. I shoved the door back and looked. What a mess. The room had been crammed for years; antique cars parts, old office furniture, leftover patio tile, camping equipment, even a windmill. Much was buried behind the scene. A mess all right but what a class room. Just the right size, 30 x 50, and more than that, the door at the other end opened to Sam's.

One 'meeting' and it was unanimous. Seminars, workshops even healing services.

It's summertime again, beginning our tenth year we stand again in another empty room. Completely empty except for some carpet swatches and a big stack of bricks against the north wall. Been there forever. My husband decided to leave them there. He'd build a fireplace.

Soon, the brick walls and concrete floors have been steam cleaned, trim painted, even the iron staircase to the second floor. I look up there and wonder. It's almost empty. Could make good lofts for sleepovers someday, maybe? Probably. But, this room we stand in is ready for another leap of faith. It needs lighting, heat and air, carpeting, sound system, video screen and certainly…chairs.

This is kenosis time, Lord. We stand here emptying and empty, waiting for your filling. Fill our hearts, minds and spirits with Your will for us, for this room.

And He did.

I Remember Ellen

Her first visit she was late. She sauntered down the hall to the room. Plopped on the center chair. Dropped her purse on the floor. After a few causal remarks (while chewing, chawing gum) she said,

"Don't really know why I'm here. Saw your article about talking with people about God, and stuff. Thought I'd give it a shot. Not much of anything going on with him, Jesus or whoever. Used to. Don't know what happened somewhere along the way. Anyway, thought I'd drop by and hear what you had to say. That's about it."

"So, do whatever it is you do."

Nearly an hour later we sat in silence. She had heard herself reveal a tragic life story of deprivation, rejection, and abandonment vomited up. We just sat. I was so weighted with empathy and sorrow that I felt useless. My objectivity was shot.

She stood up.

"G'bye."

"Want to wait a bit?"

"No. Uh, uh."

We walked slowly back down the hall together and I asked if she wanted to make another appointment.

"No, huh, uh."

At the door I asked, "Ellen, if you could have anything at all this minute, what would it be?"

No response. I tried again.

She looked at me a few moments and whispered, "Hope."

"I have hope. I'll keep it for you. If ever you want it, remember I'm holding it for you."

No answer. I watched her slump down the sidewalk.

Two weeks later she called. "This is Ellen. I'd like to make an appointment to pick up my hope."

That was the Holy Spirit at work in my weakness. The feeling in myself had been inadequacy. What do you think you're doing? You let this poor soul slice herself open and walk off bleeding. She should have been with someone more qualified than I. She was!

It was His question at the door. It was His promise of hope. His strength through my weakness to meet her where she was and go with her where she needed to go.

That brought her back to do the work, to look at her journey with God. Back with her vision to reconsider the drama, the story. And into the turning point; the willingness to change. To search for the next step. And she did!

"How did the 'Chair' story end?"

It didn't.

Hopefully it is endless.

It was.

Doris' Story

Another choice of chairs was made by Doris. Later she sent this letter to me.

"I am still processing what has happened to me. I know my life has been transformed in so many ways this past year. It's been what I consider a gradual process but I know that my spiritual life has changed 180 degrees.

The biggest change was my understanding of God. I was afraid of God. I was in no mood to surrender myself to the God of judgment and let that God have control of my life. As a result of spiritual direction I view God differently now. I really believe in the God of unconditional love. I believe God loves me and wants the best for me and I am more eager to surrender myself to this God. I believe this God accepts me where I am and wants me to continue to grow. I want God in my life and I find myself through my day turning my life over to God or laying my burdens at the cross.

I have been really aware of God in my life…literally since I began spiritual direction. I don't recall the first time this occurred, but when you Virginia, prayed for me, I felt this warm sensation travel throughout my body. And I have felt it often since that first time.

I wander a lot from God, but I slowly come back and turn my focus on becoming in God.

I only meet once a week for spiritual direction, but I want to be in communion with God on a daily basis. I want to follow God wherever I go.

Spiritual direction has taken a broken woman who had no peace, self-worth or respect for myself and changed my heart forever.

Grace, peace and love,

Doris

A Clergy Response – Another Joy

During OSL'S National Conference held in Minnesota's Augsberg College, I taught a workshop on the study and practice of spiritual direction. The following excerpts from a letter sent from a priest attendee speaks eloquently of the essence of spiritual direction from a clergy point of view:

"It was a real eye-opener to me to see that I had spent thirty years as a parish priest working in a spiritual director mode rather than a pastor or counselor. I have always seen my task as introducing people to God, and letting Him carry the ball from there. It was not my role to "fix" people, or to manipulate people into some programmed mind set that the church has preached from the top down. My parishes were always healthy when I left them in His hands.

It is my studied and prayerful opinion that unless we get back in touch with God, we will continue to wander about the desert trying to use the world's tools to solve the problems that the world's tools have created. Being a firm believer in redemptive love, I cannot believe there is a depth to which we can sink that is beyond the reach of God.

When the church gave up theology for methodology, she somehow lost contract with her source. A resource without a true Source is like a cut flower. Unless it finds new roots to a source of life, it will die."

Man on The Street

While pondering this point I remembered a man I saw downtown once in a while. My office faced the intersection so when I looked up during a pencil chewing time, I might see him standing on the curb.

He came from a shelter a few blocks west, aiming at a food pantry few blocks east of my place.

I held my breath watching him. He was a big man with a small head, neck bent down at the shoulder, able to see only his shuffling feet.

He never looked up at the street lights or traffic. He waited a bit, stepped off curb, shuffled ahead and on by my window to breakfast.

One morning I was early and went out front to water the window flower box.

He was shuffling toward me on the sidewalk.

As he came close enough to hear me while still facing the window boxes, I said,

"Good Morning."

Another shuffle and he was right behind me. He stopped and mumbled something.

I turned enough to see him. As usual, he was humped over, eyes on his shoes.

"What's that sign say?" he mumbled, head down, eyes rolled up.

"It says, Poustinia."

"What that?"

"Means desert. You come in there, someone will walk with you through the desert place in your life.

"Is there sand in there?"

"Not real sand. Just pretend."

"What's that word again?"

"Poustinia. It's a Russian word..."Pou...sti..., Pou..."

I leaned down and spoke softly right to his face, "Pou...sti..., Pou..."

He still fumbled it, until he looked up and watched my lips. We exchanged efforts several times and he finally said it softly, then mumbling, then clearer, into announcing,

"I'm no dummy! I know what's in there. I can say Poustinia. I even speak Russian."

He turned around shuffling back from whence he came.

At the intersection he stopped, shuffled off, but looking both ways.

I saw him just a few times after that. He would walk a bit and shuffle a little bit but now watching traffic.

Then, after month or so, no more, he was finished. But, he left this earth knowing how to say Poustinia, knowing "what's in there," and even speaking Russian! He was no dummy.

I wish there had been some time to explore then that still crooked back, It was less than it was but, you wonder. I would have liked to have listened to his story.

The Menningers taught us guilt can bend our back and forgiveness can straighten it.

The one encounter with the man on the street still teaches me, Holy Spirit over human spirit, over mind, over matter heals the person. The only differences are in degree.

Prayer From
Poustinia[19]
by Rev. R.D. Pelton
…and for you.

"May the risen Lord lead each of you
Into the desert of your heart,
And speak to you there in His Spirit,
And show you there the radiant mercy
Of His Father's face.
Then may He lead you
To His brothers and sisters
Who are everywhere awaiting your love."

---

[19] Catherine Doherty, *Poustinia: Encountering God in Silence, Solitude and Prayer.*
Madonna House Publications.

"Things I Have Told You"

About Paying Attention

About Paying Attention

I share a memory appearing out of a day of attempting to practice the Presence of God. Readers will realize He is always there, always available – it is we who are not.

He speaks to all of us all of the time.

But, are we paying attention?

He is steadfast...He waits.

About
Paying Attention

This particular night happened to be my turn to lead the See Christ Retreat group. Richard Foster brought members of Friends University's graduating seniors to experience retreat. My subject was "Paying Attention." He was obviously interested in the subject and asked me if I could stay after for a 'coffee chat.' For him? Is he kidding? My time was his time. Anytime. The chat was blessed with sharing, caring and a follow-up.

"Would I be busy Friday night?"

"Of course, not."

It seems he was teaching at a church west of town and would like me to come share tonight's story. Would I ever! What time and address?

I arrived early as usual. It was a big church with jammed parking lots. Inside display tables jammed the aisles. The huge auditorium was full.

Was I in the wrong place?

No, I wasn't. "Foster" was everywhere.

Must be some mistake. This was an auditorium filled with people. Not the small church classroom I expected!

The noise quieted. All seated. He was at the microphone onstage. I heard, "Is Virginia here? Where are you?"

"Where? Oh there she is!"

I recall a drum roll, assistance to the stage, him racing around, getting me in the right place, right mike, up, down, hands on the podium. Rousing applause and laughter.

I delivered my talk.

Silence. I did it. I think.

I nearly fainted when what I found out this night was the first RENOVARE.[20]

That night was also a side road in my journey, actually connected to a road I didn't even know was on the map. I was invited to teach at Friends University in a new direction called Frontiers: A lay Institute For Spiritual Growth. Many gifts would blossom forth through Poustinia.

One of them was about…Paying Attention.

The following was my presentation that night…or so they recorded.

---

[20] RENOVARÉ is committed to working for the renewal of the Church of Jesus Christ in all her multifaceted expressions. www.renovare.org

Paying Attention

"Profound dissatisfaction led me to begin trying." Laubach's[21] thought slid above my thumb and caught my attention, as though I'd never seen it before. Browsing books was a way I looked for direction, a way to move out of "profound dissatisfaction." Laubach knew that one who doesn't ask, listen, or pay attention by a deliberate act of will is not submitting to God. Laubach began to try. So, would I. In that effort, I could at least initiate the day's beginning, though never its closing surprise.

I want to share a memory with you. A memory that surfaced in a day of listening to God, or, at least, a day of desire and intent to do so. I hoped this day would be more successful than previous attempts, that it would end in a Renovare, a spiritual renewal, for me.

I share my experience in the hope that it will be a nudge, or more, in the direction of newness for you.

A most helpful aid in the discipline of listening, for me, is Richard Foster's classic, *Meditative Prayer*.[22] (It's a little book that fits everywhere - palm, purse or pocket. It goes anywhere; one of my copies has round-tripped Kansas, London, Fatima, and to the top of the Vatican in the sleeve of my umbrella!)

According to Foster, "The goal, of course, is to bring this stance of listening prayer into the course of

---

[21] Frank Laubach, *Letters by a Modern Mystic,* New Readers Press
[22] Richard J. Foster, *Meditative Prayer,* Intervarsity Press

daily experience." In every minute, moment, hour of any day – "there can be an inward attentiveness to the divine whisper." In the effort to pay attention to the "divine whisper," I could, at least, initiate the day's beginning, though never its closing surprise.

I began on this particular Friday deliberately, because it would be so simple. I would be substituting for my husband's secretary who was on vacation. He would be out of his office most of the day. There would be a few people in and out, routine Friday closures: a state report, confirming appointments. Predictable, with little or no interference. A day that could provide for reflections with Him.

And so, the morning was; asking and hearing in a sense of quiet Presence. In feeling really comfy with the progress so far, I recognized a slight tinge of pride seeing through the seams and re-positioned myself a bit.

On the second cup of after lunch coffee, I swiveled toward the window, feeling something like the cloud dozing out there. Before I finished the afternoon duties, which were few, why not have a look at the morning paper? I found a furniture sale on the back page of section one, another on page three. And so my mind wandered off to a lonely chair sitting in my living room all by itself. How cozy it could be with a little table beside it. But that wasn't on the agenda for this week. What about an estate sale? The price would be right on Friday, and sure enough the newspaper told me there was an estate sale in its final days, with my kind of furniture, only ten minutes away. Besides, the address was someone's I knew. I closed the office, leaving a note.

At the second stoplight or so, I realized I had never in my life walked off from work in the afternoon to go to a sale. I fretted about that for only a few blocks, but, "not enough to turn around and go back," I thought, with tongue-in-cheek. Easing into a parking space being vacated in front of the house, I sat there a bit, puzzling the house number. Who lives here? I don't know. The house doesn't look familiar, but I know this address.

Standing in the spacious entrance I felt for some sense of another visit. Nothing. There was a spiral staircase in front of me, winding up toward probably two bedrooms, a bath and study. There was a crystal chandelier overhead, a very special choice. Lovely. The walls, the floor in the entrance were bare, two tall chairs stood against one wall, bearing sold tags. To my right should be the kitchen and it was - just a kitchen. To my left was a step down into what was at one time a very gracious living room, empty now except for the flotsam of the final hours of an estate sale: picture on the floor leaning against the wall; drapes folded, stacked in the corner. Furniture indentations announced departed furniture about the plush carpet.

Straight ahead of me was the family room, probably flanked by one master bedroom and a bath, perhaps a second. Standing in its archway I was touched by something strangely familiar. I knew this room...

somehow. It was huge, soft, inviting. I stood still in a sense of welcome as a few bargain hunters milled about silently, mostly picking up, and putting down things on the bookshelves to my far right and here on either side of me. Mostly bare now, signs indicating small stacks of books; "Only fifty cents."

To my left was a door to the bedroom, and then a walled fireplace cuddled by a deep downy sofa with a sold-tag; a few other scattered things. A picture frame held the "Best Grandpa Award." A child's rocker yet unclaimed. The carpet held traces of the sturdy table beside the chair I was leaning on. This spot would have been my choice. From it you could see the fireplace and beyond the yard through the glassed patio. It was like all the rest of the yards this time of year, gray and brown. Trees, leaves, swing, dying flowers, tall, gray and brown.

I stepped into the master bedroom, empty except for a king-sized bed and was greeted by feelings of intimacy, even privacy being violated, and yet I felt included, not invasive. Who had lived here? I had to know and would go at once to the attendant and ask. Then I heard someone else ask and the response: "Faith and Bob Richards lived here."

Bob and Faith Richards? Finally a memory came into view. I sat down in the chair and let it live again.

It was a fall like this one, when all your favorite people are in town. Seminars, workshops, conferences, but as the excitement mounts, so does the problem. How are you going to manage all this? You can't make them all. A friend and I decided to whip this dilemma by dividing up speakers and exchanging tapes; at least we would get some of each of everything. So in the aftermath, I was in my kitchen, doing the things you do in late afternoon.

I began listening to the first in the set of tapes. I had been to this man's conferences, read his books, listened to his tapes. The familiar voice made for easy listening. But as I settled into what I presumed was going to be routine dinner preparation, I was interrupted by a "Pay Attention To This!" feeling.

I rewound the tape. He was sharing the healing of his physical heart condition and I was suddenly riveted. I had not been praying with anyone with a heart condition, was not aware of any in my family or anyone around me that would cause this quick grab of attention. I rewound the tape again. There was a spurt of adrenalin, an alertness that I have known before when suddenly confronted with the knowledge that this is information I will need. I listened again. And, then I waited...until the next afternoon.

"My name is Faith Richards," the voice on the phone said. I have been referred to you by our mutual friend Sue, to pray for my husband." He was in intensive care with heart failure, was comatose, and according to the physician, probably had only hours to live.

Driving to the hospital was frightening. The familiar warmth in my hands was intensifying into painful heat and numbness; I could not feel the steering wheel. The parking garage was a welcome sight. In the waiting room outside intensive care, I recognized the anticipation on the face of the one who must be Faith Richards. We greeted one another, prayed quietly together, and went to Bob's bedside. His eyes were closed. I spoke his name. He did not respond: His body was silent. His spirit was not.

I invited the Holy Spirit into this place, into me. Into Bob. I thanked Him for the privilege of standing in the gap. Asked for his openness to the Lord's healing touch. I placed my hands on his chest, imaging his heart as it was created to be, as the Lord wanted it to be. And waited...

In a while there was a twitch beneath my hands, a jerk, and a change in the rhythm in the heart. His wife squeezed my shoulder. The monitor echoed the motion beneath my hands. In a while, it began to quiet. There seemed to be a peace coming into the rhythm. And there was stillness. And he was being healed. I spoke his name again. He slowly opened his eyes, and I said to him, "The Lord is healing you. Receive Him, receive Him," and he closed his eyes again.

The monitor leveled.

He was healed.

I waited for what seemed an appropriate time and quietly left the room.

Late that night began the first of many calls to come through Faith's bedside phone in her master bedroom. Other times she called from this chair. We rejoiced together, offered prayers of thanksgiving and praise for His healing love. Our spirits came together and were in His in this room and in that room, in the days to come. And then on homecoming day there was another tone in her voice.

"Bob's heart is functioning normally but his kidneys have begun to fail. Would you please come again?" I was quite surprised to hear my voice say, "No. This time, you go. God's healing flows through His Love. You are a deeper vessel for your husband than I. Go to him. Intercede for him in the same way."

Later that night, she called, the sound of a child-like faith in her voice, the quality of obedience that must surely be the Lord's delight. "I prayed for him in the same manner you did," she said. "His kidneys are functioning properly."

During his recovery we talked about changes going on in her: a mixture of discontent and enthusiasm welling up in her, a hunger dashed with a sparkling joy, the need "to be about my Father's business" in a more defined way. A healing prayer group of her own, perhaps? Aha! That was it! I suggested, *Three Together*,[23] solid teaching for beginners, a springboard. She was delighted with the new direction stirring in her. And off she went. Our paths went on their separate ways...until today.

The sales attendant appeared, in my reverie, and pleasantly reminded me the sale was over. Everyone else was gone. I apologized, walking with her to the archway; then I had to ask, "When did Mr. Richards die?"

---

[23] Freer and Hall, *Three Together,* Harper, New York.

She turned to me in surprise and said, "He didn't die...she did."

Out of the stunned silence betwcen us, I finally said, "I would like something tangible from this place."

I fumbled two or three books on the nearest shelf and then held in my hand *Three Together*, Faith's book. Inside was her name, little notes, turned down corners.

There were names of people in her prayer group, meeting times, underlines in special places...the most priceless possession in this room. And it belonged to me for fifty cents.

Back home as I tucked it into a book shelf with other treasures, I patted it gently and then, "Oh, Lord! I've not called your Name since lunch!"

It seemed He smiled at me and said, "Then, I called YOU...again."

"Things I Have Told You"

About The Rock

About

The Rock

I want to share my quiet place with you. I found it a long time ago, and now again.

I sat quietly, eyes closed, still, with nothing to say except, "I just want to be with You, Lord."

After awhile I saw a curtain. It hung from sky to earth and north and south horizons.

In my mind's eye, I walked toward it. It was sheer as chiffon with a luminous texture of some sort. I parted it and stepped inside. Standing on the walking path of soft dirt over hard ground. I was twelve years old, knee length dress. Tanned legs, and barefooted: squishing warm silt between toes. A summer day.

The path went east ahead of me about one half mile and wound around a hill on the horizon. On either side of the path were beautiful fields, basking in sunshine, wildflowers here and there. The field was bounded on both sides with assorted sizes of hills. To the right side of the path was a pond of crystal-clear water. On the left side was a huge round rock , about one-half foot tall, and five feet in diameter. Basking in sunshine. There were too worn spaces where people must have been sitting together forever.

I was to go to the Rock.

As I began, Jesus, on his earthly ministry, rounded the far hill onto the path toward me. I was not at all surprised.   We smiled, waved, and onto our meeting place: the Rock.

We sat close, his arm around my waist.   No audible words, just knowings, exchanges, thoughts, and feelings. Most of all joy. The joy of just being with. Sounds of silence.

When the time was up, we went back from whence we came. We stopped for a wave and smile.

Back to the curtain. To where I came.

In the days following, life was simpler. Some concerns were gone.

As it began to fade, I knew for sure, the 'being with' showered His amazing Grace.

In the Grace were gifts, life to live, love to love.

My quiet place and its sounds of silence had become a ritual through many years. Sometimes neglected, or wandering off, but always to return.

A few months now, after my husband's death, grieving was moving normally and as expected until the day I plummeted to the bottom of the pit. In a split-second of objectivity I recognized the danger point I had seen in others; I didn't care. I just didn't care.

By this time in my life, I've had lots of losses like so many people have. I've had my share, but I've never lost a husband before. So, this has been quite different. I did go to the six week classes on grieving and did all the things that I was supposed to do. So when different feelings, emotions or experiences come to me,   I'm aware that this is part of the process.   That this is the way you get through this, and it will take much time.

I've had some depression the first couple of weeks. And I expected that. I knew what it was when I saw it, and about how long it would probably last, and what would help me to get through it and I did. But these last two weeks have been different. I started to have a depression one day and just slid down and down and down. And there wasn't anything I could do to stop it. A couple of days later I was still down. I could not get up. I did all the things I'm supposed to do, and said all the things I'm supposed to say, and it didn't matter.

I really didn't care much whether life went on or not. What else is there? I knew it was getting out of control, and I was determined to get myself out of it.

So, for the first time in my life I spent the fourth of July alone. I decided I was going to get up the morning of the fourth, stay alone all day long, while all the family is out doing something else; just leave me alone, I'm going to get out of this. So I got up in the morning about six a.m., or a little after, and had some coffee. Then I gathered up my books, stuff that I wanted to read, different selections of the Bible that I wanted, writers that I especially liked. Then I sat down in my chair to work through the grief process.

I prayed, I did contemporary prayer. I tried about four or five different types of prayer that I knew about. And the silence, the listening. All the things that ordinarily would have begun a movement out of that depression.

I heard, "Come back to the rock."

He was waiting for me. Hugged me close and asked, "Do you know where you are?"

"No."

Waving his other arm across the view, he said, "This is the 23rd Psalm. These are the green pastures. Those are the still waters. No evil in this valley. I am with you, I hold you, I comfort you, My love feeds you all the days of your life."

"I am your physician."

He is your physician.

"Things I Have Told You"

Epilogue

Epilogue

Mother once told me that when each of my brothers was born their first word was "Hi"!

Mine was, "Why"?

How do you find out anything without "Why"?

I don't know either.

Where and who I am now is extension, out of all the years before, and now the prelude of what's to come.

Why were my dolls sick? How did they get well? These are the questions that taught healing.

Then the boys' messy feet and lumpy heads that were great strides in healing of mind.

Above those discoveries peeked questions about emotions. You could say emotions over mind over matter?

Then the healing Power, the mysteries of Holy Spirit over and through spirit, and emotions over mind over matter.

All these seemed to move from the childhood "why" into the endless maturing, into and through Holy Spirit of God, through Jesus Christ.

On my night table rests a gift from Mother. She was dying with Alzheimer's when she made it for me in art class. It is a plaster piece with a reading from one of her favorite books, Proverbs. It reads:

"In all thy ways

acknowledge Him

and He will

direct your paths."

When I do, He does.

The gift of ministry that flourishes through all others is the gift of spiritual direction. There comes a swirling awesomeness through and in all gifts that His Love is all and in all.

One gift that we have not known in spring and summer is a new retrospect. We can see our journey now from the grandeur of mountaintops, the howling desert and its soothing sand. The peaceful plateaus and terrifying cliffs. The confusing intersections and the clear highways.

We see the shoulds and the aughts that didn't matter anyway. We see an overview of death into life, through the glass a little bit more clearly. It's the one season that prepares for the winter of rest that precedes the new spring, the ultimate healing.

He has walked barefoot with me in green pastures. Hanging on to the sail in the stormy sea. Dried my tears in the wind. Held me close in the ecstasy of Love that is only His.

Finally, from Chardin's, *Hymn of the Universe*,[24] a part of his closing prayer. Also, mine and perhaps will be yours:

---

[24] Chardin's *Hymn of the Universe*, English translation from St. Joseph Place, London. Copied by library Virginia Theological Seminary, Alexandria, VA.

"Jesus-Omega, grant me to serve you,

to proclaim you, to glorify you,

to make you manifest to the very end,

through all the time that remains to me of life,

and above all through my death.

Lord Jesus, I commit to your care my last active years,
and my death.

Do not let them impair or spoil the work I have so
dreamed of achieving for you.

The grace to end well, in the way that will best advance
the glory of

Christ-Omega: this the grace of graces.

I continue to go forward to meet You who comes.

Amen."

All these years of discerning my journey by attentiveness to its design has led me into my little corner of His kingdom, St. John's Episcopal Church, Wichita, Kansas.

It's my 86th birthday. As I peruse and ponder all the "Things I Have Told You..."
...the years cuddle me.

There's a
Place
For you

Here in
Space
For you

When it's
Time
For you

I will
Bring you
Home.

Journal 1975

Notes

To order additional copies of this book,

"Take A Scroll and Write About…

Things I Have Told You"